TAKE BACK YOUR *Pearls*

NADIRAH GAGE

A 90 Day Journey to Taking Back Everything That The Enemy Thought He Could Steal

"This is the season to
TAKE BACK YOUR PEARLS."

TAKE BACK YOUR PEARLS
Copyright © 2021 by enGage Life LLC

All rights reserved. No part of this book may be reproduced or transmitted in any form or by any means without written permission from the author.

ISBN 978-0-578-31168-5

JOURNEYS

PREFACE

PEARLS

INTRODUCTION

REPENTANCE

FORGIVENESS

OFFENSE

BOUNDARIES

CORRECTION

HUMILITY

DISCIPLINE

OBEDIENCE

AUTHORITY

IDENTITY

ACCEPTANCE

SUBMISSION

AWAKENING

PREFACE

This book would not be possible without my Lord and Savior, Jesus Christ. Without Jesus, I would not know what it means to walk in abundant life. I would not know what it means to be loved by a Father who loves without limits, and I would not know what it means to know that someone went through death so that I could experience life.

I did not grow up in church. I was not raised knowing much of who Jesus was aside from some scriptures that I would hear and some hymns that my grandparents would sing. Today, this journey continues and I am learning about the fullness of Him and being full in Him. I am embracing the endless capacity of his reckless love and standing on the truth that I am loved. I am standing in my identity in Him to know that there is a need for me that is bigger than me.

Through depression, toxic relationships, financial strains, suicidal attempts, and being a young and single mother; I have been able to witness the love of Jesus. A man who is more than a Lord and a Savior to me; but also, a Father. A Father that I did not come to know until I reached a place where I wanted to give it all up. A Father that kept pressing forward through the pain that he had to endure because He wanted to TAKE BACK what the enemy thought he could steal. He bled and sweat, was beaten and mocked, and died a horrible death because he knew the greatest secret ever. He knew that through his death the enemy would be defeated and that meant that the enemy could no longer steal what Jesus already paid the price for.

We were all bought at a price. As women, we might stumble on this truth. At times, it might even confuse us when we use this idea of being bought in the wrong context. We can think that our worth is found in how much a man can financially provide for us. However, Jesus shows His love for us and our worth in Him so much that he gave up His life for us to rise. It was His blood that paid it all and was big enough to cancel every assignment of the enemy.

The hard reality is that we have been silenced and hurt by people who should have been covering us that we forget that God has already taken us back. Instead of walking in freedom, we allow the enemy to take root in our thoughts and our hearts, which then overflow into our actions. Without realizing, we begin to identify ourselves with characteristics and mannerisms that are opposite of what God says. Our circumstances then become the foundation of how we operate in our daily lives. However, our circumstances do not identify us; Jesus does.

Jesus knew who He was as He walked the Earth but He did not have to showcase it. His words were powerful enough. In fact, they were so powerful that even when the devil aimed to tempt him, he did not need to succumb to the requests of the devil although he had the authority to do so. He knew who He was because Jesus knew His Father.

My prayer is that you will know your Father in a way that allows for freedom and intimacy. I love my husband and he does an amazing job as a husband and fathering our three children, however, even my husband will fall short at times. However, our Father, who is perfect, is still fighting for you today so that you can have the authority to face the enemy to take back what is not his!

The words in this devotional come from my perspective. These words are backed up by Biblical Scripture. I understand that everyone's situation varies and I encourage you to ask God to lead you as you read and go through this 90-day journey.

COMPELLED TO LOVE

A Poem by Carolyn Grignon (My Mother)

No laws of attraction required
The mere fact that we belong to Him
We were His from the beginning of time
Miraculously designed and exceptionally gifted
He designed us according to His plan...

PEARLS

"Don't throw your pearls to pigs! They will trample the pearls, then turn and attack you." (Matthew 7:6 - NLT)

God opened my eyes to two things in this verse. The first thing was a pearl and the second thing was a pig. It's easy to see that these two things do not mesh well together. A pearl is a beautiful object that can be worth thousands and a pig is an animal that is often seen as dirty and not worth that much. However, they both do begin with the letter "P." Yet, in all seriousness, there was a reason why Jesus said these very words. Why would a person want to throw their pearls to anybody, let alone a pig? Sadly, Jesus speaks this because he knew that anyone of us would be capable of making this mistake. The consequence wouldn't be just that once the pearls were thrown that they would be trampled but that we also would be attacked. A pearl is formed because when a parasite tries to attach itself to it, it creates a defense mechanism. Through the tests and attacks, a beautiful and shiny object is created. It withstands the tests and what forms is something beautiful. Our pearls are the things in our lives that hold value, those things that sometimes we have had to fight for so that they could take form, and those things that God has had to protect so that we would not let them go. These are things that we cannot throw at pigs or people who won't appreciate them because of the value that they hold. They become a part of us and when we give them away, in the end, we will also be attacked.

As women, we are created to take back our pearls if we have thrown them aside so that we can walk in the beauty and the fullness that God desires for us to walk in. We must stand assured knowing that regardless of what irritant might come at us or what parasite tries to attach itself to us, that when we fight against the enemy then we can come out stronger!

INTRODUCTION

The second message that I ever preached was titled, "Take Back Your Pearls." Over two years later, I had no clue that the same message would speak volumes to me. My husband and I transitioned from a ministry that we knew for our first few years of marriage to be a part of a church plant. We believed that our time in that place was up and that we heard God tell us to go. As we believed this, we faced much opposition and pain. We were unfriended on social media and it seemed as if we were cast aside because of the decision to go. This was a season where I felt angry, used, taken advantage of, underappreciated and undervalued. I felt as if what I had sown was being uprooted. I felt that the enemy had stolen what God had given me; which was my peace. This was the time where I began searching and asking God questions that I never knew I had. Why was I angry? Why was I hurt over a ministry that Stefen and I moved to Orlando to be part of? Why was I beginning to resent a ministry that we once loved? I struggled with the reality that this was a major shift, not just physically, but also emotionally. The major problem was that I looked around at the many factors but I failed to look at myself, my faults, my wrongdoings, and my role in all of this.

This was a season where God was calling my husband to something that He placed inside of us, but I did not see the entire picture, I only saw a piece of it. I let the enemy take root inside my heart and those roots grew branches. I held things in and became so bitter with silence about how I felt towards all that was happening in that season. Instead of confronting my feelings and people, I communicated them to my own self and battled with my own self out of fear of not being heard or appreciated. My identity became wrapped up in serving people more than I served God and my validation came more from man than from the One who created me so when these relationships shifted, I felt that a part of me died.

The reason for this book is not to say that people are bad, or that they are out to get others, or that they are evil because we ALL fall short. It is to say that I gave my pearls, those things such as my time, my peace, and my heart to so many other things before asking God if it was okay. I believe that this is something that many of us do. We give away the things that are most valuable to people that do not know how to handle things that are valuable. Although they might not be terrible people, they are still people. Because we fail to look at our own selves, our own faults, and our lack of priorities then we risk playing the victim instead of taking responsibility for our part in all of it.

However, this is the time where we will learn how to fight to take back our pearls. This is the season where we will prioritize God so that He can show us what to give, when to give it, and who to give it to. I will warn you that as we go through this growing process, it will hurt and it will not be as easy as we declare it to be. However, there are some things that have to die so that new things can grow and there are some things that we have to break in order for them to be mended. This is my desire for you.

You have the ability to TAKE BACK YOUR PEARLS!

REPENTANCE

A little over ten years ago, I learned about this word repentance. We were doing a book study as part of a young adult ministry that I served at and the author broke down this word in a way that I never truly understood prior. I knew that this word was associated with people asking God to forgive their sins. However, through the text that we were reading, I learned the deeper meaning of this word and the value that it held.

Knowing that God was a God that forgave our sins was so refreshing. Learning that God was a God that desires for us to literally hate the sin that we commit required me to see God in a new way. Yes, He is the God of love and the God of forgiveness and the God of grace but He is also the God that desires us to hate what can separate us from Him, and that is sin.

During my young adulthood, there was the immature part of me that saw big sins and little sins and I began to categorize my wrongdoings into compartments. I would stop drinking and would stop fornicating but I would not hate it if I saw my brother or sister doing it. I could still be connected to them and go out with them and party with them as long as I was not the one 'participating' in it. I didn't really hate the sin, I just wanted to remove some sins so that God would bless me out of my partial knowledge of obedience. However, I neglected the truth that I still carried unforgiveness and jealousy and lack of concern for those around me who were struggling spiritually. I found it hard to love people past the hurt they inflicted on myself and others. This meant that I could not walk fully in the love of Jesus. How could I love my neighbor as myself if I did not hate the sin that my neighbor committed? Or how could I think I was living right just because I had hidden sins that people were not able to see?

God sees it all and He sees the real us!

He sees the real us and calls us to repentance through the way that He loves us. Let me share it to you in an example using my husband, Stefen, and myself. There are times when I get upset with Stefen and because I am angry, I can be rude towards him. In my mind and my heart I know that I am wrong and there are times when I let the anger continue. However, because Stefen understands love God's way, he will apologize and love me despite my anger. This action of how he loves me, leads me to repent. It leads me to want to be a better wife, leads me to hate the anger that I sometimes can have, and leads me to start taking up the roots of where this anger stems from. Oftentimes it is not because of him, but because something in my past, that I have yet to overcome, was triggered.

I am thankful for Godly marriage because it is my mirror. It exposes the things that we can hide from the world but not from one another. Some couples won't make it because knowing the inner parts of a person can be scary and sometimes people do not know how to handle it. On the other hand, people hide from the mirror and wear cover up to be someone that they aren't, only for years later to hear their spouse saying that they never knew them.

For those of you who are not married, that is okay because for all of us, God is our mirror. He knows our iniquities and He sees what is in our heart, even before we say anything. If He is all knowing and He still loves us, then as daughters we can talk to Him about the sins that we are dealing with and ask Him to help us hate those sins. When we can understand that we are all sinners saved by grace, we can understand that there is not any big or little sin, that we are not above anyone else, and that we are all in need of a Savior, Jesus, to do what we could not do ourselves...pay the debt for our sins.

Taking back the power of repentance, which begins with the love that God has for us, is the first area that I want us to journey through. For some of us women, we feel that we have been blamed since the fall of Adam and Eve when Eve ate the fruit. For others, it seems that we have been held down by society's standards when compared to men. Even in some cultures, our rights have been stripped from us or even taken away. As women, we strive to wear so many hats while still aiming to walk in grace and love. With all the opposition that we may face, we still push forward. Yet if we are real with ourselves, we get tired, overwhelmed, and sometimes even angry. However, God has called us not to be weary! Even when we are weak, His strength is perfected.

Here is a great example from the Bible from John 8:3-11:

The teachers of the law and the Pharisees brought in a woman caught in adultery. They made her stand before the group and said to Jesus, "Teacher, this woman was caught in the act of adultery. In the Law Moses commanded us to stone such women. Now what do you say?" They were using this question as a trap, in order to have a basis for accusing him.
But Jesus bent down and started to write on the ground with his finger. When they kept on questioning him, he straightened up and said to them, "Let any one of you who is without sin be the first to throw a stone at her." Again he stooped down and wrote on the ground.
At this, those who heard began to go away one at a time, the older ones first, until only Jesus was left, with the woman still standing there. Jesus straightened up and asked her, "Woman, where are they? Has no one condemned you?"
"No one, sir," she said. "Then neither do I condemn you," Jesus declared. "Go now and leave your life of sin." This text encourages me on so many levels. Too often we have heard that men can do things that might bring about a reputation and be celebrated, however, when a woman does then her reputation

precedes her in ways that are degraded. This was what happened in this text over two thousand years ago. The woman was caught IN the act of committing adultery and sadly ladies, some of us would be talking about this woman today. However, Jesus did not care about her sin, He cared about her heart and wanted her to hate the sin so much that she would leave that life. His love for her brought her to a place of repentance and shifted her to cling to Jesus instead of the sin that she was entangled in. We all have the ability to TAKE BACK the gift of repentance!

Jesus declared. "Go now and leave your life of sin."

__DAY 1__

The word repentance translates from the Greek verb that is transliterated as the word metanoeo, which means with an understanding or with an exercising of the mind. When a person repents, they have to make a conscious change in their mind and their soul to know that the sin in their life is bad. Once they are aware of this then they can pursue the actions needed in order to turn away from the sin.

Acts 2:38 says, *"Peter replied, "Repent and be baptized, every one of you, in the name of Jesus Christ for the forgiveness of your sins. And you will receive the gift of the Holy Spirit."*

Repentance was not intended for one person. Peter says here that repentance was for everyone. This was the same Peter that denied Jesus three times after he walked with Jesus.

What does repentance mean to you?

Why do you think that Peter urged everyone that was present to repent and be baptized?

What is the greatest gift that a person receives when they repent for their sins? What is the Holy Spirit to you?

DAY 2

Within our worldview, we can believe that there are little sins and big sins. However, if someone tells a small lie, does that mean it is still a lie? Of course! So if we sin, whether we think it is big or small, are we still sinning? There is only one way to define sin and that is doing the opposite of the eternal law of God. If I go over the speed limit by one or twenty mph, I am still breaking the law. What happens when we start looking at big sin and overlook small sin is that we risk believing that the small sin is not sin at all. Galatians 5:9 reads, "*A little yeast works through the whole batch of dough.*" So although sin might seem small, it can become a greater problem later. To clarify, I am not saying that different sins do not impact us differently. I am saying that when we realize that sin is what separates us from God, then we can become more aware of the sin that is present in our lives.

Read Matthew 5:27-29. What is Jesus saying about sin?
Do you tend to compartmentalize your sin and think that there are bigger ones and smaller ones in your life?
How can you make a decision to not compartmentalize the sin in our lives? How can the Holy Spirit guide you?

DAY 3

In chapter 3 of Acts in verse 19, Paul says:

"Repent, then, and turn to God, so that your sins may be wiped out, that times of refreshing may come from the Lord."

When we repent, we turn away from our sins and turn to God. He is the only person that can help us to remove the sin from our lives since He was a man who walked this world and did not sin once. It can be so easy to be caught up in sin and not realize that we need to repent. However, be encouraged in the truth that repenting allows us to depend on God more than ourselves and because He is a God of love, He desires us to come to Him to find freedom and peace.

What sins are in your life that you are finding it hard to turn away from

Are you trying to turn away from the sin in your own strength or are you pulling on the strength of God?

What does Acts3:19 mean personally to you? What is the reward that comes from repenting?

DAY 4

We all have people in our lives, who are like mirrors. They can see our blemishes and our imperfections and sometimes they can be the ones to expose them to us and even help us to clear them up. However, we know the greatest mirror is God. When we know His word then we can line ourselves up to it and see that we do fall short, however, we can still be encouraged to know that each day in His presence, we can get better.

James 1:23 - 25 says, *"Anyone who listens to the word but does not do what it says is like someone who looks at his face in a mirror and, after looking at himself, goes away and immediately forgets what he looks like. But whoever looks intently into the perfect law that gives freedom, and continues in it—not forgetting what they have heard, but doing it—they will be blessed in what they do."*

What does this verse mean to you?
What are some blemishes that you or other people see in your mirror that you need God to help you clear up?
Why is it so important to have God be your mirror and why do we need to look at this mirror daily?

DAY 5

As women, we love hard and we love deeply and sometimes within our lives, we have seen that love has not always been reciprocated. When we look at who Jesus is, He is love. His love is what kept Him on the cross for crimes that he never committed. His love was so massive for us that he was mocked, beaten, died, and buried...BUT the beautiful thing was that Jesus did not stay in the grave. He rose! Yes, love caused Him to experience so much pain but it also called for others to experience so much freedom in Him. One of my favorite Bible verses is I Peter 4:8 which says:

"Above all, love each other deeply, because love covers over a multitude of sins."

It is the love of God that allows us to walk in repentance because He loves us without boundaries or limitations.

In what ways have you witnessed God's love in your life?
Do you love God enough to lay down your sins for Him?
How is the love of God in comparison to the love that people have shown you throughout your life?

DAY 6

In the text of John 8, Jesus came to the place where a woman was because He was called out by a group of Pharisees and teachers of the law. Sometimes, we can be like these people and desire for others to repent, while not looking at our own selves.

Matthew 7:3-5 says:

"Why do you look at the speck of sawdust in your brother's eye and pay no attention to the plank in your own eye? How can you say to your brother, 'Let me take the speck out of your eye,' when all the time there is a plank in your own eye? You hypocrite, first take the plank out of your own eye, and then you will see clearly to remove the speck from your brother's eye."

Today, I want you to reflect on this verse. What does this mean to you?

Ask yourself and be honest about whether this is something that you do at times. What triggers this type of thinking?

Reflect on whether this is something that you are capable of doing towards a certain person or group of people. If you do, how can you make efforts to do better?

DAY 7

REFLECTING

Jesus declared. "Go now and leave your life of sin." (John 8:11)

Think of when Jesus said this to you. Were you obedient and if so, are you obedient to this today?

As women, we are encouraged to Take Back our gift of repentance but also to encourage others to do so as well. In what ways are you sharing the gift of repentance with others in your life?

What are you able to take away from this section on repentance?

25
TAKE BACK YOUR PEARLS

FORGIVENESS

Early in my Christian walk, I saw God as a God who was extremely loving and forgiving. There were even times that I felt that because of the way that God loved and forgave us, in spite of our shortcomings, that He could easily be taken advantage of. I believed that people who knew they would be forgiven easily could keep on making their mistakes with no thought of changing. It was like that person who accepts a toxic relationship where the 'toxic' person keeps apologizing and the 'weak' person continues to take them back. However, I wasn't aware of the true meaning of forgiveness. I was looking at it through my lens and viewpoint. Really, I was looking at it as if God should have a cut-off point because He would risk being taken advantage of, just like that 'weak' person in that toxic relationship.

You see, I was pushed over, mocked, made fun of, and taken advantage of both verbally and physically. Even through all of that, I forgave easily and continued to allow people to hurt me, without voicing how I felt. This left me feeling as if I was weak...as if I didn't have a backbone or a voice; and this is how I later viewed God. I looked at Him like I did myself. In my eyes, he was too loving, too forgiving, and too kind because He forgave so much. I didn't fully comprehend who God was or the power that He walked in until I understood how it takes a strong person to forgive another without holding their faults against them. God goes even further! He actually took our faults and died on the cross so that our faults and wrongdoings could be nailed away. I was over here thinking that God was like me but I am not anywhere on God's level! Yeah, I might not have thrown people's faults in their faces, however, that did not mean that I did not carry them in my heart. Not only did I carry them there, I let them impact other relationships that would later come.

Anything that starts off small has the potential to grow into something big, especially when it has not stopped. When we don't deal with unforgiveness, it will begin to deal with us to the point that our relationships are formed from a place of caution more than a place of concern. Many of us can be blinded to this and think that we are coping fine. However, when left untreated, unforgiveness can cause pain towards the people who want to love us and cause a wedge between us and those who desire to push us to become the person that God has called us to be. Because God knows who He is and knows who we are, He knows that we need forgiveness so that He can fully operate in our lives. He does it so that we can have the best example of what forgiveness looks like. God isn't weak and He is not being taken advantage of. He is showing us the best example of love.

Let me share a story. For a long time unforgiveness caused me to believe that my husband didn't love me deeply. Of course I knew that he loved me in general and still, I couldn't believe that he loved all of me with my shortcomings, my mistakes, and my areas of brokenness. I thought that there could be a cap on his love because I saw the cap of the world's version of love. Before we were married, I even saw a cap, or a limitation, of his commitment that I equated to his love for me. When I met my husband, I was at the age in my life where I was ready for a serious relationship that would lead to marriage. My husband, who was younger than I, started to feel like he was too young to settle. When he voiced this, it opened my heart up to hurt, confusion, and fear. Some of those feelings still lingered even after God told him that I would be his wife. Even though I believed that God said it, and even after the counsel that we received, and after the assurance that was given over and over; I started to love out of fear. A fear of one day believing that my husband would wake up and think that he made a mistake; which was being with me. So although I loved my husband so much, the possibility of him hurting me within marriage laid the foundation for walls of insecurity that stemmed from unforgiveness that I had towards him and others. I couldn't fully give my heart to this amazing man who loved me at my worst because he hurt me when he wasn't at his best.

I needed God to do major heart surgery on me. Years of unforgiveness had caused me to develop a stony heart condition. This stony heart condition is mentioned in Ezekiel 36. It is a condition that God desires to fix by replacing the heart of stone with a heart of flesh. Many of us have hardened hearts with soft smiles and our hearts are saying things that our mouths have been trained not to say. This was me! For years, I had harbored hurt and I had not forgiven those who hurt me. It didn't matter if they were still in my life at that current moment or not because at the end of the day, the iniquity of unforgiveness was taking up space in my heart.

Sister, it doesn't matter how much you aim to keep the fire burning in your marriage, or how much you keep pouring out in your career, or how hard you serve in your ministry and calling; if you have a hard heart then eventually it will begin to show. Before it does, we have to know that we have solutions. For me, it started with this word that we know as surrender. I had to get to a place outside of my own head, a place away from the anger I felt, and a space different from one that wanted God to punish those who hurt me rather than to restore them. That place was my prayer closet. I was home, alone, and vulnerable and cried out to ask God to help me forgive and to forgive me for all that I had harbored. I prayed, I cried, I worshipped and as I continued to make time to do this, I would begin to feel a release. I saw myself as God's child and I also saw others who wronged me as God's children too. Like I could be forgiven, so could they. God loved me in all of my mess even more than my husband loved me in all my mess; and let me tell you that man loves all of me, but this showed me that I could love people in their mess too.

I felt that my heart was free from a chain that started off as a small link that grew into something later because I did not take care of it. Imagine a weed that has been left unattended. You can pull it up and it may be caught under another link of weeds and you continue to pull it up after realizing there are more clusters of weeds on top of one another. Go to the root, and pull up the root, only to find that there is one major cluster of weeds attached that is destroying your plants and your good soil all because it was not attended to and overlooked.

I encourage you not to overlook the root of your hurt. I urge you not to gloss over that feeling of unforgiveness or offense that may take root in your heart. Go to God unashamed and ask Him to teach you how to forgive, how to love, and how to walk in humility. Ephesians 4 calls for us to get rid of bitterness, rage, anger, and even slander; all of which I battled with! It does not stop there! It also says that we are to be kind and compassionate with one another and to FORGIVE one another because God forgave us. This really hit me. I have children and I desire for them to look at the good choices and the good part of my character because they are a part of me. However, what is even greater is that we belong to God. We are made in the image of God so we have to reflect the heart and the image of God. We have to forgive as He forgives. This does not mean that we cannot have boundaries and it does not mean that toxic people should continue to spill their toxins into your atmosphere.

However, it does mean that we cannot hold a person's faults against them and expect it not to take space in our hearts. We have to forgive and release and allow God to handle the person because after all, He is still their Father.

"I will remove from you your heart of stone and give you a heart of flesh."

DAY 1

The word forgiveness is very complex and often misunderstood, however, for purposes related to this devotional, I will sum it up as pardoning someone for the wrong that they have committed. When we look at Jesus, we can see that he wants us to forgive those who have hurt us. It does not matter how many times that they have wrong us, we are still called to forgive. Luke 17:4 says: *"Even if they sin against you seven times in a day and seven times come back to you saying 'I repent,' you must forgive them."* No one said that forgiving someone is easy. However, in the eyes of Jesus it is something that we must do. The number of times that someone sins against us does not matter. We are still called to walk in the power of forgiveness. This does not make us look weak; it makes us look like the image that God created us in.

In your words, describe what forgiveness means to you?
Why do you think it is important to pardon someone who sins against you?
Forgiving someone can be equated with someone who is weak but how can forgiveness actually show strength?

DAY 2

How many times have you held someone's faults in your heart but you haven't told them? As women our hearts could be saying something that our mouths never say. This lack of communication can lead to distorted relationships and internal issues that we struggle to put into words. However, when we release to people how they have wronged us then we can give them the opportunity to be aware of their actions and also an opportunity to be sorry. Yesterday we looked at Luke 17:4 but the verse before that says: *"So watch yourselves! If your brother or sister sins against you, rebuke them."* Basically, this means that we have to look at ourselves. We can't harbor things in our hearts. Instead, we have to take back our voice and speak up when someone does something wrong. Otherwise, we will continue to walk around smiling with a bleeding heart that has the potential to hurt people who can help heal us.

Are there any faults that you are holding in your heart?
How often have people wronged you and you have not followed what Luke 17:3 says and rebuked them?
Even though forgiving can be difficult, why is it beneficial?

DAY 3

In chapter 6 of Matthew in verses 14 and 15, Jesus says: *"For if you forgive other people when they sin against you, your heavenly Father will also forgive you, but if you do not forgive others their sins, your Father will not forgive your sins."* When we forgive others when they sin against us, then we are mirroring our Father who forgives us all the time. The greatest commandments are to love God with all our heart and to love our neighbor like our own selves. Walking in forgiveness allows us to follow these commandments since forgiveness shows that we love God as well as our neighbor.

What unforgiveness are you finding it hard to let go of?
Do you believe that God still accepts your faults when you don't forgive others? Why or why not?
In what ways have you applied Matthew 6:14 -15 in your life? Are there any instances where you have not?

DAY 4

We all have experienced being hurt by people, especially those who love us. Sometimes the hurt can be intentional and other times it might not be. Regardless of what people have done, we have to be aware of the effects that unforgiveness can have on us. Ephesians 4:31-32 says:

"Get rid of all bitterness, rage and anger, brawling and slander, along with every form of malice. Be kind and compassionate to one another, forgiving each other, just as in Christ God forgave you."

What does this verse mean to you?
What are some things that can attach to our flesh when we do not forgive?
How does kindness, compassion, and forgiveness look to you and how can you fully walk in them?

DAY 5

As daughters of God, we are called to forgive but that does not mean that it can be easy for us to forget. I shared how before I married my husband, I hadn't forgiven him for how he hurt me nor did I forget it. In fact, it ruled a big part of our relationship. However, Hebrews 8:12 says that God will forgive our sins and He will not remember them anymore. What this means is that He doesn't hold us to our mistakes but He pushes us to be better. We are ALL sinners saved by His amazing grace. Throwing our sins into a sea of forgetfulness means that we are no longer bound by our shortcomings. However, when people hurt us it can be hard to forget. The burden can follow us for years but when we pay more attention to it then we risk that iniquity having more dominion over our lives than God does.

List some people that you have forgiven but whose actions you haven't forgotten.
Do you have a hard time praying for those people? If so, why?
What are some things that God has forgiven you for? Are they of lesser value than what someone has done to you?

DAY 6

In the text of Ephesians 4:25-27, Paul shares how we must tell the truth to our neighbor because when we allow even one day of unforgiveness to harbor in our hearts, then we can give the devil an open door to have a foothold over our minds.

"Therefore, each of you must put off falsehood and speak truthfully to your neighbor, for we are all members of one body. In your anger do not sin: Do not let the sun go down while you are still angry, and do not give the devil a foothold."

Today, I want you to reflect on this verse. What does this mean to you?

Ask yourself and be honest about whether you speak truthfully to someone when they hurt you. If this is something that you do not do, what is keeping you from doing it?

Reflect on a time when you allowed unforgiveness to go on for more than one day. How has that made you feel when you thought of the situation or the person that caused the hurt? Now, write about what steps you could have taken differently and why.

DAY 7

REFLECTING

"I will give you a new heart and put a new spirit in you; I will remove from you your heart of stone and give you a heart of flesh. And I will put my Spirit in you and move you to follow my decrees and be careful to keep my laws." (Ezekiel 36:26-27)

Think of these verses. What are the stony places in your heart that God wants you to replace with flesh?

As women, we are encouraged to take on the Spirit of Christ. We can only do this when we have a heart that is soft enough to love the way that God loves. When we love the way that He does and His Spirit is within us, we can walk in ways that are pleasing to Him. In what ways are you sharing the gift of forgiveness with others in your life?

What are you able to take away from this week on the topic of forgiveness?

39
TAKE BACK YOUR PEARLS

OFFENSE

I did not come into the knowledge of what offense was and how it impacted me until I became more committed to my walk with God. I knew of the idea of people taking offense for the things that people said or did, however, I never looked at the viewpoint from an internal perspective. Rather, it was summed up as something that was done externally, whether intentionally or unintentionally, to hurt me.

The sad thing about this mindset is that it looks at everyone else as the enemy or as wrong but fails to look at the internal triggers or even the spiritual battles that are taking place within the person who is carrying the offense. In addition, because the focus is often on people who we see on the outside, the person who is walking in that offense can feel that they are justified to walk in anger or even malice towards the person or people who have offended them. In many cases, the wrongdoings done towards a person can begin to stack up without anyone being aware that harm is being done. As the offense builds up greater, it leaves little room for grace and creates a wall of justification around a person's heart. *When offense grows, grace has no room to flourish.*

I was that person who walked in offense. I had a limit on my grace towards others, which today sounds so ridiculous because how could I have a limit on something that was not mine!

However, how many of us are guilty of this? We allow offense to put a restriction on the grace we give others as if we are the ones who created grace in the first place. When the Bible talks about grace, it talks about it being a free gift from God and not from man. In my human flesh, I was hoarding grace as if I owned it and extending it when it was convenient for me to do so. Sure, I might have had valid reasons to feel hurt or pain by others, however, I did not carry the right of letting that hurt or pain weigh so heavy in my heart that it shackled the free gift of grace given by the Father..

Some of us are walking around making people pay for the gift of grace that was freely given to us and the truth is that God knows when we do this. Imagine owing someone a large debt and they told you not to worry about it. You were given the gift of not having to pay something back. Now imagine a short while later you come across someone who owes you a smaller debt and your response to them is that they have to pay you back. However, someone gave you enough grace to say it is okay; don't worry about it. Jesus talks about this very thing in Matthew 18 and it is linked to unforgiveness because offense breeds out of unforgiveness and making oneself seem better than others. The man in Matthew 18 was given grace and forgiveness but did not extend the same to another. It is time for us to do a self-inventory of the offense that we are carrying. It is time for us to take back what we are holding over others and be thankful for what has already been removed from over our heads that we did not deserve.

Offense is visual. When we carry offense, it shows in our relationships. It shows in how we treat our brothers and sisters. It shows in the way that we love those we do life with. It shows by the way we treat people whom we barely know. It is not a discreet thing. I remember when my husband and I were taking our pre-marital classes and how we learned that when someone carries offense towards a person then if that person walked in a room then their whole demeanor would be off. Anger and agitation would be present regardless of how discreet that a person would try to make it. Although nothing might be said, you can still feel the offense in the room.

We have to be honest and be real with ourselves and the people who offend us. This is a work in progress for me, however, just because it takes work doesn't mean it is the hardest thing to do. It is harder to walk in offense than to walk in freedom and peace but like I said before, it takes work. Like repentance, it takes a heart check for us to see if we are harboring any offense. Heart checks are something that we should do often. When David asked God to search him, it was because David knew that the only person that truly knew what was in his heart was God and that the only person that could fix his heart was God. David knew that if a fence or a wall was built up around his heart then he could not have a heart that loved what God loved. If David did not love what God loved then he would be disqualified from being known as a man after God's heart. So, I encourage us to ask God to search us consistently. As daughters of the king, we have to decide whether we want to be women who have a heart that is towards God's heart or women whose heart is towards our own desires and justifications. I am not saying that we will never get upset or get hurt by others by any means. However, if and when those situations of hurt and pain arise then we have to posture ourselves to go through the healing process and the forgiveness process so that we do not carry that hurt and that pain and that offense into other relationships that have the potential to grow and be fruitful. As daughters of Christ, we cannot have a cap on our grace and do not have room in our hearts to harbor anger that we too often justify because of the actions of others. We can rest assured that God fights our battles and cares about the condition of our heart as we face life's hurts; but as He fights for us, He will also have the final judgment and His judgment will be just. It is time to allow Him to be our Defender and not let any potential offense that we carry to take root in our hearts. When justification of actions that are opposite of Christ take root in our heart then our heart will love from that justification. That is a scary place to be. We love because God loves not because of what is justified to us or not.

When we walk in offense, then we carry that spirit of offense. This means that the viewpoint that we look at people or situations from becomes dysfunctional. The spirit of offense leaves no room for Holy Spirit because the Spirit of God does not carry offense. Ephesians 4:2-3 says, *"With all humility and gentleness, with patience, bearing with one another in love, eager to maintain the unity of the Spirit in the bond of peace."* This Scripture speaks of unity and the bond of peace. Offense, on the other hand, causes division. While we might think that we are dividing ourselves from another it is really that we are dividing ourselves from God since offense keeps us holding on to unforgiveness and leading us to walk in our own gospel.

As Take Back women, we can no longer allow offense to build up walls around our heart. We can no longer look at every situation as a battlefield for us to become offended. We can no longer put a limitation on the love that we show towards others because of the freedom that offense has had in our mind. It is time for us to have conversations, to give people the benefit of the doubt, and to know that man will fail us but God's Word will always remain and His love for us will always endure. We all have been offended and we all have offended someone at some point of our lives, however, now is the time where we have to fight for forgiveness, grace, and love.

"....maintain the unity of the Spirit in the bond of peace."

DAY 1

Because we live in a fallen world, things will offend us. However, when a person walks in the spirit of offense, then they have little room to walk in the gift of grace. The gift of grace is not something that we can buy or create but it is given to us by God. Knowing that Jesus was persecuted means that we are not exempt from people attacking us. Yet, even with people hating him, Jesus still continued forward. If we are not careful then offense will slow us down. We have to be able to acknowledge when someone offends us so that we can walk in sincerity and love. Philippians 1:9-11 says, *"And this I pray, that your love may abound still more and more in knowledge and all discernment, that you may approve the things that are excellent, that you may be sincere and without offense till the day of Christ, being filled with the fruits of righteousness which are by Jesus Christ, to the glory and praise of God. (NKJV)"*

How would you explain what offense is to another person?
How has offense hindered you from walking in grace?
Looking at the verse about, why is it important to walk in love and sincerity?

DAY 2

Because of our own mind's limitation, we can sometimes look at everyone else as the reason that we are offended instead of looking at how we might have offended someone else; even without us knowing. If I borrowed something of yours and did not return it, would you be angry towards me although you did the same thing to someone else that let it go? We have to look at ourselves and our mistakes and not be overly focused on what someone else should or should not do, according to our perspective. We might be able to understand what is right and wrong, however, we have to be able to look within ourselves to take back the hold that past offenses have on us.

Read Matthew 18:23-33. What does this parable speak to you about offense?

How often have you been offended by something that you have also done at some point in your life?

Knowing that you have also offended others, what action steps can you take towards keeping offense from building up in your heart?

DAY 3

Romans 3:23-24 says, *"For all have sinned and fall short of the glory of God, being justified freely by His grace through the redemption that is in Christ Jesus..."*

This verse doesn't say that one or two have sinned but that all have sinned and have fallen short of God's glory. Although we all fall short and we all have sinned, we have the gift of free grace so that we do not have to stay in that sin. We can get back up. When offense resides in our heart, that means iniquity lies there as well. We have to remind ourselves that God's grace is free and redeems us from all sin. His grace and forgiving love can wash away our iniquity.

Some of us have experienced traumatic things. What are some offenses that you feel that you just can't let go of?
God's grace is important to extend to others. How are you extending grace to others as well as yourself?
Walking in offense means that iniquity can lay in our hearts. What does that mean for our prayer life? (Psalm 66:18).

DAY 4

Offense is something that can be noticeable. It shows up in our conversations, by how we treat other people, and even by the things that we say about others that they do not know about. Most importantly, God sees the offense and God knows that offense can lead to something worse when we do not deal with it. When God spoke to Cain in Genesis 4:6-7, here is what he said to him: "*Then the Lord said to Cain, "Why are you angry? Why is your face downcast? If you do what is right, will you not be accepted? But if you do not do what is right, sin is crouching at your door; it desires to have you, but you must rule over it."*

This was the response after Cain was offended because his offering did not get the kind of recognition that his brother received. It was so bad that it led to him killing Abel.

Why do you think Cain was so mad at Abel?
Can you recall any time where you have been offended but you really were just upset about the choices that you made?
As women, how can we stay aware of the offenses that we have that could be covered up by insecurities we carry?

DAY 5

As offenses come, we have to know how to experience healing. I believe that healing takes place through many forms, such as counseling and talking about different experiences. I also believe that God's Word plays the biggest part in our healing process. But just like with counseling, you have to be willing and able to apply the lessons in your daily walk. We are called to bear our crosses each day, and while it might be challenging, we have to do the work. We are daughters and His word says in Matthew 11:28, "*Come to me, all you who are weary and burdened, and I will give you rest.*" Sometimes we have to be reminded that Jesus wants us to come to Him and coming to Him takes action!

Why is healing so important?
Do you tend to run when it comes to complete healing? If so, what are some reasons now for you to stay through it?
If the verse above shows Jesus telling people to come to Him for rest, will he be your first resort from now on?

DAY 6

When we have a heart that is after Jesus, it means that we lay our rights down. We might experience hurt and offense, however, we can also experience a renewal of our heart. David was hurt and he also hurt people, but David had a heart that was after God and a heart to be a King. As we read the Psalms of David, we can see how he poured his heart out because he knew that nothing could be hidden from God.

Psalm 139:23-24 says, "*Search me, God, and know my heart; test me and know my anxious thoughts. See if there is any offensive way in me and lead me in the way everlasting.*"

Why can this prayer be a scary prayer at times?
What are some things in your heart that you keep hidden from others but that God is able to see?
It is important to see if we are offensive beings. Reflect on things that you have done to offend others and be open to asking for forgiveness and forgiving yourself as well.

DAY 7

REFLECTING

As women, let us be encouraged to Take Back the gift of forgiving others by walking in grace. We aim to do this so that offense does not cause us to stumble or enable us to adapt to a way of life that looks nothing like Jesus.

How are you stewarding this gift of grace so it is not hoarded from others?

Paul says in Ephesians 4:2-3 that *"With all humility and gentleness, with patience, bearing with one another in love, eager to maintain the unity of the Spirit in the bond of peace."*

What will this specifically look like for you?

52
TAKE BACK YOUR PEARLS

BOUNDARIES

Growing up there were certain places that I was allowed to go to. These places were places that my parents would consider as safe. In the same way, my parents would allow me to have friendships that were safe in their eyes. If for any reason any of those relationships or environments gave any signs of being unhealthy or unsafe, then a boundary was immediately put up.

My parents were able to easily identify if a person or place seemed unsafe when that could see what took place on the exterior. However, when it was hidden, it was a bit more difficult to tell. The thing was that although it might have been hidden, I still knew what was unsafe or not based on what they taught me over the years. However, although I was aware, I did not always know how to put boundaries up. I was a people pleaser and afraid of leaving people out, so I continued to please people. I began to allow their actions to influence mine. Over time, I would start to become so frustrated with myself; which led me to becoming frustrated with the relationships around me.

As I became an adult, I had to learn to experience the need to put boundaries in place for myself. I had to learn to remove myself from stagnant and toxic friendships that produced no fruit. At one point my parents created them for me but as I grew, and am still growing, I was able to create them for myself. This could be some of you ladies. Others have put boundaries on you and now you are learning how to create the necessary boundaries for yourself. As you are navigating through this, I want to make it clear that boundaries are not to be confused with isolation. I believe that we all need community and we all need to do life with people. I also think that there are times when we are going through things and sometimes say that we are putting boundaries up but we are really isolating ourselves from people. The enemy loves us to be isolated. If he can get us alone and distanced from the people that sharpen us with the word and encourage and hold us accountable then he can achieve his plan of division. However, when we use wisdom, we can know what boundaries that we need to have in place and which friendships that we need to keep close to us. This is not isolation from people but rather putting people in their rightful place as it relates to their access to you.

I am a wife and a mother and so my husband and my children have full access to me. I am called to be Stefen's wife and so that means that we walk in oneness. We have complete access to one another. I am also called to be a mother to Nahla, Seven, and Nia and so they will have access to me as their mom. As they get older and they get married and have their own families, they will still have access to me with boundaries in place. Why? Because as they are one with their spouses and called to lead their children then that means that I cannot overstep my role, although I am their mother. Boundaries are not always a bad thing and while my kids might have access to me as their mom, they will never have the same access to me that Stefen has.

There is a boundary in place. As women, whether we are married or not, we need to really take a look at the access that people have to us and make sure that it is not interfering with our roles as God's daughters. For those of us who are married, we also have to ensure that other people are not having more access to us than our husbands because when that happens that is out of order and out of God's will.

Sometimes boundaries are motivated as we walk through forgiveness. We touched earlier on forgiveness and how we are all called to forgive just as God forgave us. Knowing this, that doesn't mean that walking in forgiveness means that we also walk in forgetfulness. While we can release the hold from the pain that they inflicted on our hearts, that does not mean that we can always forget what they did towards us. Our minds can still remember, and because of that, we have to make a daily and conscious decision to choose not to hold their faults against them. It is sometimes easier said than done but when I look at every nasty and ugly thing that I did to sin against God, I cannot even remember all that it was and the beautiful thing that when it comes to God, He throws it into the sea of forgetfulness. To us, we may not be able to forget but we also do not need to hold that person's sin against them. My husband said something so profound by saying that people look at our wrongs as cards stacked against us but God gives us a clean slate. For us, I believe that a new slate mindset can happen when we allow that person to still be loved, while praying for them, and still allowing boundaries to be in place as God guides us.

Boundaries are things that are extremely important as it relates to relationships. Those relationships that are new and ones that are in need of healing and restoration can benefit from proper boundaries. In the book of John, it is stated that Jesus knew all people and knew what was in a man. Jesus knew their heart even better than they knew it and as Jesus lived His earthly ministry, He only went where the Holy Spirit enabled him to go. He shared the gospel, encouraged his disciples to do so, and told them to dust their feet off if people reject the gospel since they were rejecting God. In addition, boundaries are needed because we do not know what is really inside a person's heart. Sometimes there is necessary time that is needed to see how a person may handle a situation or even space needed to see how others may handle when you are going through things. With proper space in place then we can strive for healthier relationships. I gave people too much access to my heart, my home, my finances, and other areas. I believe in ministry this is something that many people have experienced and that is sometimes the risk taken as we love those that God sends. However, there needs to be a space in between where God is in our presence and we are listening to Him in regards to the people that we need to be around and the ones that we need to proceed with caution. The point of taking back your pearls means that before you even give anyone your pearls, you have to know if you are giving them to swine or not. We know that I Corinthians 15:33 says, *"Do not be misled: "Bad company corrupts good character."* This means that we have to know which company is bad for us because it can corrupt a person's character. In addition, we also have to be aware if we are carrying the corrupting character.

My husband and I were taught this concept of boundaries, which we also teach to couples. Before moving to Florida, I thought this was a common thing, however, we learned from Ros and Deen Allen's way of teaching. Although it was very uncommon, it was also very important. Boundaries gave a man and a woman space to learn one another as God was at the center of guiding where the relationship would go. As impulsive beings who have the desire for communion that was placed in man at the start of creation; it is not accidental that many of us would skip over boundaries and go all in. However, when this happens, men and women who like each other can quickly find a pathway to lust. As this door opens, then God now is on the outside trying to get access back in and He should have been on the inside of their relationship through its entirety. Even in relationships and ministry, we have to seek God to know that there is a time and a season and a place for who we do life with and when God is left out of it then someone will end up with a broken heart.

BOUNDARIES...we all need them!

"Do not be misled: "Bad company corrupts good character."

DAY 1

When thinking of a boundary, we can think of an area or a place that we cannot have full access to. This space might be something that we see on a consistent basis or have been familiar with. In either case, we have to know when and why we need boundaries. As we are led by the Spirit, God gives us revelation so that we do not create boundaries based off of unforgiveness, a hard heart, or offense. What we do know is that when we are in relationships that are toxic and are not producing fruit, boundaries are needed. This does not mean that we operate in hate or outside of love but we should measure our relationships according to God's standard. John 15: 1-2 says, *"I am the true vine, and my Father is the gardener. He cuts off every branch in me that bears no fruit, while every branch that does bear fruit he prunes so that it will be even more fruitful."*

What is Jesus saying in this passage?

Are there any relationships in your life or things that you are attached to that are not bearing fruit?

Being that Jesus is the true vine, why is it important for Jesus to be at the center of your relationships?

DAY 2

There are times when we need to have alone time with our Father so that we can engage in a relationship with Him; where we can know His voice and seek His face. There are also times when we can be encouraged by and encourage the community that God has placed in our lives. Because of these factors, we need to discern that while boundaries are needed, we cannot get to a place of isolation where neither God nor our community is keeping us accountable. Isolation can be a dangerous place if we are not being led by the Spirit. Jesus went away to be with the Father and also gave His time to serve those that He was called to serve.

Luke 5:15-16 reads, *"Yet the news about him spread all the more, so that crowds of people came to hear him and to be healed of their sicknesses. But Jesus often withdrew to lonely places and prayed."* As Take Back ladies, we need to know when we have to take back our time alone with our Father and know when to be available to serve those we are called to serve.

What can you take away from the passage in Luke 5:15-16? How can you discern knowing that there is a time to serve and a time where you need seclusion?
How can you ensure your seclusion is healthy?

DAY 3

Having boundaries is helpful for order. When we think about order in the Kingdom, God is always first. For those of you ladies who are married, your husband would come after God and your children after your spouse and then the church. Sometimes if we are real, we can put our children before our spouse, or our ministries before God. Since we are pulled in many directions, we have to do order checks. In some seasons, our attention might be pulled into an area more than others but we still have to fight to maintain that correct order while being aware of the access that we give to people. This is challenging even for me, but God left us with this comfort in His word.

Hebrews 4:16 says, *"Let us then approach God's throne of grace with confidence, so that we may receive mercy and find grace to help us in our time of need."* When we need the help to do this, we can go to God. He has removed the boundary.

List the order of priority in your life currently. Be honest.
Why is it important that God is number one?
What can happen when we give people more access than God or our spouse or even our children?

DAY 4

As God leads us to put boundaries in place, we have to ensure that we are not holding that person's wrongs against them.

There are times when we might gossip about someone who wronged us and we put up a boundary without communicating to that person. However, we can communicate to everyone else about that person. When we do this, we are allowing gossip to be part of our character and forgetting that God's grace can restore.

When I think of the woman at the well, she was known by her actions. I am sure that people had things to say about her. She went to the well at a time when others wouldn't. She did so because other people had boundaries towards her...BUT...Jesus extended grace! He didn't talk about her to others. He told her the truth, in love, to her face. Take some time to read John 4 and reflect on her story.

Have you placed a boundary on someone without telling them? If so, were led by God, anger, offense, or fear?
Are there any relationships where you should have extended more grace?
Why is it important to allow the Holy Spirit to lead you to having the right conversations as needed?

DAY 5

There are times when we want to jump all in with people so we invest our time and our hearts into those relationships. Sometimes these can turn into great relationships and other times they can result in a lesson learned. When we go all in, we have to have realistic expectations that sometimes people might fail us just like we will do them since we all fall short. Because of this, it is good to allow space as we get to know a person, while being open to take time to understand their heart posture.

I Samuel 16:7 says, *"For God sees not as man sees, for man looks at the outward appearance, but the Lord looks at the heart."* We can easily judge someone based on their appearance and actions and be misled so it is important to seek God because he knows what is in a person's heart that their mouth has kept hidden.

What takeaways can you take fromI Samuel 16:7?
How do you set boundaries when meeting new people?

Do you give people the benefit of the doubt more or do you give the space to get to know them more? What are the pros and cons of both?

DAY 6

Sometimes boundaries are formed as a result of being hurt and we need time to process the events that have hurt us as we heal from them. As we navigate through this process, we also have to navigate through the reality that there is a possibility that we will remember the actions that hurt us. While we do not have to hold a grudge, boundaries can be helpful in those instances where we need to create a space as a shift in trust occurs in the relationship. If this is the case for you, consider putting boundaries in place so healing can take place. As you do, be honest with all parties and walk in the truth that God wants to deliver you from your hurt.

Psalm 34:18-20 says, *"The LORD is close to the brokenhearted and saves those who are crushed in spirit. The righteous person may have many troubles, but the LORD delivers him from them all; he protects all his bones, not one of them will be broken."*

What is God saying to you through this verse?
Take some time and write out and journal the memories of relationships that have hurt you?

As you create boundaries, how can you differentiate between boundaries that are needed to heal and ones that began from offense?

DAY 7

REFLECTING

"Do not be unequally yoked with unbelievers. For what partnership has righteousness with lawlessness? Or what fellowship has light with darkness?" (2 Corinthians 6:14)

As women, we are encouraged to Take Back our knowledge of having boundaries God's way while still serving the people that we are called to serve.

In what ways are you placing boundaries in your life?

Are your boundaries communicated in a way that is loving and not a result of anger or offense?

What things and actions are you able to take away from this section on boundaries?

CORRECTION

My parents were very big on correcting their children. The way that they would correct us would vary from one to the next. Nonetheless, correction was a major staple in our household. In their eyes, correction was needed so that we were aware of what we did wrong and also so that we would be more likely to remember the consequences of our actions. Throughout our lives, we may witness some people getting corrected by their parents and other cases where the parents might be more passive. In addition, we might see people who correct in love and those who correct in anger. While the outcomes of the way that we correct might be different for others, it can be safe to assume that when correction is done without love and grace, it can lead to resentment. On the other hand, when correction is done in a way that is loving and graceful, there is a better chance that the person in need of the correction is more receptive to it.

We all are in need of correcting. None of us walk in perfection or know everything. However, it becomes a scary place when we carry ourselves in a way where we cannot receive correction and where we think that we know the answer for everything. This is especially sad when we are in a position where we lead in ministry but because of our titles we think that we are too high for correction. This is an unhealthy place to be so we need to have solid people around us who can correct us in love but also have grace to walk us from the areas of fault to the areas that will bring fruit. As a wife who is married to a pastor, sometimes I am seen as a person who should always make the right decisions and be even tempered. And while that is something that I strive for, it is also something that I have failed at. I fall short, I have lost my cool, I have made bad decisions but I am thankful for the people who have corrected me and have encouraged me to walk better. If I would not have heeded the correction and thought of myself as better than I would not have been able to walk towards a place where I can overcome those same shortcomings. Correction has the opportunity to allow us to thrive because we can be better than where we were. We need people around us who can correct and build us and not condemn and tear us down.

When we look at Jesus, we see someone who loves but also someone who also corrects. Hebrews 12:6 says, *"The Lord disciplines the one he loves, and chastens everyone he accepts as his son."* I have two daughters and a son, whom I love. However, even though I love them, I correct and discipline them. I can see things that they cannot see and understand how certain actions can lead to certain behaviors and consequences. On a higher level, God knows everything and sees all so when He corrects us and disciplines us, it is for our good. When we have the right people in our lives, that we are accountable to, we can know that when they correct us then it is for our good. Some of these people can open our eyes to seeing blind spots that we cannot see. As God leads you to them, don't run from correction when it might seem hard and don't limit yourself from accessing correction because you think that you are good without it. We ALL need correction.

Proverbs 15:32 says, *"Those who disregard discipline despise themselves, but the one who heeds correction gains understanding."* When we heed correction then we can access understanding. On the other hand, when we disregard correction then it harms us even more. I understand that some of us ladies have been corrected in the wrong way. Some people might have even abused their power and authority as they corrected us. This happened to me as well. Even still, we have to learn to heed God's voice and obey God's will and follow as He leads us. As we receive correction from the right people, we want them to be those that will not pacify our behavior but will not tear us down either.

Unfortunately, some of us ladies get into this space where we want an audience or a cheer squad. This might be one person or it might be a few. These are those who will allow you to dump, allow you to gossip, allow you to sin, allow you to stay stagnant, and do nothing to correct you. Sometimes you might even keep these people around because you want to stay stuck. I encourage you to break free from that. If there is more foolish talk and behavior leading the relationships that you are in than the Holy Spirit, then you need to have a correction check. God's word will help you. His word is sharp. It is also clothed in love. 2 Timothy 3:16 reads that *"All Scripture is God-breathed and is useful for teaching, rebuking, correcting and training in righteousness."* Scripture is used for teaching us and also for rebuking and correcting and training us. We need to pursue righteousness above all things. In order to pursue righteousness, we also need to pursue correction. Does correction seem painful? Yes! However, although it might feel painful to go through, that feeling will not last forever. Hebrews 12:11 says, *"No discipline seems pleasant at the time, but painful. Later on, however, it produces a harvest of righteousness and peace for those who have been trained by it."* When we are being disciplined, it might seem unpleasant and painful at that moment. However, later on it will be a benefit to us. There is even a benefit of righteousness and peace when we are trained from correction. While we are training, it might seem painful. As someone who ran hurdles in track, I had to train. As I trained, I was also corrected on my form and my speed. I wasn't the fastest runner so at times I would feel the pain of correction. I would tell myself that I was slower than the other girls and didn't have the gift of running. Even still, my coaches would keep me in hurdles. They would still have me run on the varsity relay team because even though it was painful at the moment, it pushed me to work harder. They were not mean about my speed but they did hold me accountable and pushed me every time I stepped out on that track. I remember we even trained with the boys and it was that training that helped me to perfect my form and increase my speed. It produced a reward for me that was not in the form of a medal or going to the state meet, but a reward to see that other people believed in me when I didn't even believe in myself. It produced a feeling of being loved because other people saw something in me that I could not see. Now imagine how God sees us. Through His correction, it allows Him to mold us into the person that he desires. When He does this, the person that we grow into is far greater than what we could have done on our own without his correction.

As Take Back women, we have to be open to being corrected and also be willing to correct others as needed. There might have been times when we know someone needs to be corrected, however, we feel that it is not our place or may not want to open the door for an argument to arise. We also might be walking on eggshells of not wanting to judge someone or seem that we are better than they are. As we walk on these eggshells, we then can begin to pacify the issue or ignore it altogether. We aren't called to say something to everyone but there are people that we are called to correct. Even more so, there are people that we can be an example to. We can show them responses and actions that are appropriate and ones that are not. When we carry love for our brother and our sister then we also carry the desire to correct them from a place of love. Just like our sins hurt God, let their shortcomings hurt you as well and just like God corrects us from love, let your correction encourage them to do better.

"All Scripture is God-breathed and is useful for teaching, rebuking, correcting and training in righteousness."

DAY 1

When it comes to receiving or giving correction, it is better when it comes from a place of love and truth rather than a place of anger and manipulation. When correction is done from a place of love, then it can aid in building a person up rather than tearing a person down.

Hebrews 12:6 says, *"The Lord disciplines the one he loves, and chastens everyone he accepts as his son."* We are God's children, and as a good Father, He disciplines us as He loves us. If He was not concerned with correcting us, then we could act in a way that would never identify us as His children because there would not be any correction for us to know how to act as His own.

Why is it important that love is the foundation of correcting?
Have there been any times where God has disciplined you and you have felt that it was not fair?
After reading Hebrews 12:6, why do you think that the Lord disciplines his children?

DAY 2

Sometimes we have been torn down more than we have been built up. As a result, we can be hesitant to take feedback from people who have been sent to our lives to help us grow into the women that God desires us to be. Correction has the opportunity to allow us to thrive because it allows us to have the opportunity to go further than where we currently are. Proverbs 27:17 says, *"As iron sharpens iron, so one person sharpens another."* If we are not being challenged by sharp conversations and disciplined through God's Word then we risk becoming dull. We should desire to be in a community where we can build one another up through God's word so that His sharpness can be perfected in us.

Do you have people in your life that you trust to correct you in love? Why or why not?

As you read Proverbs 27:17, what examples of relationships come to your mind that exemplify this?

What fears, if any, do you have of having relationships where transparency and correction is present?

DAY 3

As Take Back women, some of us are in positions where we have titles and positions and lead others. Others of us might even be in environments where we correct and teach people how to tailor their actions and how to conduct themselves. As a wife, a mother, a sibling, a ministry leader, teacher, and coach; I find myself in that role often. However, I am not exempt from getting corrected and I need to have people around me who will do just that. When we are in positions where we are leading, that means we are also in a position where we are submitting.

As leaders, we might not have all the answers or guidance. However, we can take delight in knowing that God is the answer. He will send people who are called to teach and correct us. Regardless of your title or your position, receive the correction that you need to walk in your full purpose.

List at least 3 women that you trust to correct you. Why do you trust them?

Why do you think that women in authority might have trouble with being corrected?

Proverbs 15:32 says, "*...the one who heeds correction gains understanding.*" What does this mean to you?

DAY 4

Can you recall a time where you knew that something was wrong, however, you continued to go along with it? Can you recall knowing that someone was acting in a wrong way and you did not have enough courage to stand up against it? I have been there. Sometimes I did not have the words to say or I didn't want to be the party pooper, however, I learned to care less about what man says and stand more on what God says. After all, it is His word living inside of us so when people reject His word, they aren't rejecting us but are rejecting God. (Luke 10).

As Take Back women, it is time to take back our authority of speaking God's word, even in situations where it might not be popular or even accepted. 2 Timothy 3:16 says, *"All Scripture is God-breathed and is useful for teaching, rebuking, correcting and training in righteousness."*

According to 2 Timothy 3:16, what is the importance of Scripture? How often do you stand on God's word to speak out against something that you know is not right?

What would hold you back from speaking God's word?

DAY 5

My husband often challenges me when it comes to correcting my children. I remember when I would have a hard time correcting them. When I would, I would then make a joke out of it. In short, it was hard for me to stay committed to the correction that needed to take place.

Sometimes if we are not careful, we can give flimsy correction and have a challenge holding people, who we are called to correct, accountable. We can make jokes or pacify the behavior and it can do an injustice to those people who genuinely trust us to lead and guide them. However, we have to keep in mind that when we correct in love, we don't need to give off mixed signals. We can be firm, we can disagree, and we can correct even if it is uncomfortable.

What are some ways that you correct that shows you are serious and loving towards those that you are correcting? What can happen when we give mixed signals in our corrective approach?
Read Galatians 6:1-2. How will you correct others going forward?

DAY 6

I remember getting corrected by my husband. It hurt. Not because of the way that he did it but because he knows me and sees things that sometimes I might not always see.

This is how God is to us. He sees all of us, even the things that we can't see. He is El Roi and because of that we know that His correction comes from a place that will build us up and also pierce the very sin that needs to die within us.

Before you reflect on day 7, I want you to be aware that every word of correction is not of God. When it is, it might hurt, but you will feel the love and the truth behind it as I felt when my husband corrected me. I have been in that place, where a corrective 'word' was spoken over me and I was too afraid to rebuke it. It was a word that shackled me and took someone seeing that word in the Spirit and praying against it. Do not be afraid to rebuke as I was. Even Jesus had to tell Peter to get behind him and so can you. Fear was something that bound me, however, God's love for me was something that freed me. I pray that as you enter into deliverance from words that were not from God; that you allow God's love to permeate any fear that might exist throughout this journey.

I John 4:1 (NIV) says, *"Dear friends, do not believe every spirit, but test the spirits to see whether they are from God, because many false prophets have gone out into the world."* How often are you testing spirits around you?

Meditate on Matthew 16:23 (NLT) reads, *Jesus turned to Peter and said, "Get away from me, Satan! You are a dangerous trap to me. You are seeing things merely from a human point of view, not from God's."* Are there any words of correction that you need to rebuke? If so, spend some time today casting those words down.

Going forward, how can you identify if a word of correction is coming from God's view and not man's?

DAY 7

REFLECTING

"No discipline seems pleasant at the time, but painful. Later on, however, it produces a harvest of righteousness and peace for those who have been trained by it." (Hebrews 12:11)

As women, we are encouraged to Take Back our desire to receive correction. When we do, it produces something far greater than what we see. In what ways are you limiting opportunities of being corrected in your life?

Are these limitations a result of experiencing correction that was painful or put you down?

What is your love language of correction? Meaning, how are you more likely to be receptive to it? What can be produced in you out of correction from God?

… TAKE BACK YOUR PEARLS

HUMILITY

When I think about the life of Jesus and the way that He walked in humility so that we could have a better life, I get encouraged. I get encouraged knowing that I mattered enough for Jesus to walk the Earth; the very thing that His Father created by the sound of His words. I am thankful to know that someone loved me enough to do what no one else could ever do; save me. When I think of the beauty of it all, Jesus was the most powerful man to walk the Earth and He was the humblest man as well. In the environment that we live in, we see there are so many people who are in places of power, however, they allow that power to build up their pride and status in a way that can leave the people that they are supposed to be influencing hurt or lost. However, Jesus sets the example. Philippians 2:7-8 says, *"Instead, he gave up his divine privileges; he took the humble position of a slave and was born as a human being. When he appeared in human form, he humbled himself in obedience to God and died a criminal's death on a cross."* Jesus humbled himself to take the position of that of a slave. While other people are forced into slavery, Jesus gave up his rights to take this position. No one else could do it but Him. Out of obedience, He gave up something that some of us hold onto so tightly; our position. He died a criminal's death although He was innocent. He didn't fight back with words, He didn't use His power, He didn't even try to finesse His way out of what He was sent to do. Out of Jesus' obedience and humility and love, He did what He was instructed to do even when it was hard.

Humility is that attribute that many people say that they want to have, however, when we are found in situations where our rights override the rights of the Father then we can find it hard for our humility to take a front row seat. Expectations, offense, unforgiveness, and pride can sneak its way in the form of false humility if we allow it. We then begin to follow the wrong direction and with the wrong intentions. However, if we are following the direction of the Holy Spirit then we have to follow the direction of humility. There will be times when we have to take on a position lower than what we think we should because there are a group of people who we would never see or reach if we are too far up. The beautiful thing about Jesus is that when He humbly came in man form to reach all, He had to go to a lower place in order to get to the place that He already left. Let me break that down in case that went over your head. Jesus left the throne to come in man form to die on the cross. After the third day, He was raised up with ALL power in His hand and is still seated at the right hand of the Father. Whenever we are called to serve or called to an assignment, we should never leave to go up. If we are in the presence of God at all times then that is our high place! It does not go higher than when we are in the presence of God. This is why it is necessary for us to be in a posture of humility because pride is not an attribute of God's Spirit. Jesus did not come to Earth out of selfishness, but out of selflessness, He gave himself away. I remember asking myself too often, why I had to do things that were 'beneath' me. However, we have to differentiate what this word 'beneath' means. If we are talking about 'beneath' as in it is not producing any fruit in your life then that is not your portion. However, if we are talking about 'beneath' and it is a task that God has assigned for us to do but because we are not comfortable or are too prideful then we consider it as 'beneath' us. However, this is a wake-up call that as Take Back women, if it is from God, then it is not 'beneath' you but there is some humility that comes with the process. Our assignments are not based on our personal gain, but just as Jesus came to save those of us who were meant for hell; we have to know that we are called to give hope to a generation of men and women who we need to value above ourselves because they don't know their value when they are not in Christ. However, when we can walk in humility and love on those in spite of how they look and in spite of how they even have treated us, then you are walking in the ways of Jesus. c (NIV). If we are not valuing others above ourselves then we will struggle to be in that high place with our Father because that is what Jesus was sent to do!

Humility will clash with our pride because when pride exists, then disgrace exists too. It can seem as if we are elevating to a certain place, however, when a lack of humility exists then we really are not elevating. We might be seeing a different view but that does not mean that the view is from a higher perspective. We might be going higher in man's standards but we have to be honest as to whether we are going higher in God's eyes and going higher in God's means laying some things down, such as pride.

Pride comes from a lack of knowledge, a lack of love, and a desire to be someone that you are not. When we see the account of the fall that occurred in the garden, it was pride that enticed Eve to desire something else that looked better than what she had. However, it was a lie because pride dresses up in the lies of the enemy that says we can be better off if we care about ourselves and what we can get from the world more than what we already have been given by our Father. Do not let pride drive you but instead embrace the wisdom of our Father. I know that sometimes we can feel insignificant. I know sometimes that it can feel like our hands are tied to so much. I know that sometimes it feels worldly satisfying to respond in a way that does not bring honor. I want to encourage you to walk in the humility that God has dressed you in. It looks amazing on you and women need to see other women walking in a way that can pull others up, even higher than themselves because it takes that pull from you that can allow them to walk into things that they never would have if your pride kept you from extending your hand. James 4:10 tells us that humility will lift us up and the amazing thing about that is that it can lift others up to God as well. Do not despise humility! With humility comes wisdom because it is in that place where we humble ourselves that God uses us in a way that we never could be used if pride drove us. In humility, you can be filled. In humility, you can have peace. In humility, you will face trials just as Jesus faced them as well. However, in humility you can be like Jesus and finish your assignment so that you and others can be lifted up with him. Remember that when God calls us to an assignment, nothing is considered small because he is the Creator of it all. He is all powerful and even in his might; he still chooses humility. This is what he was clothed in and he desires for us to take back our humility and to wear it well!

"Do nothing out of selfish ambition or vain conceit. Rather, in humility value others above yourselves "

DAY 1

When we look at the life of Jesus, we see a man who walked in humility. He sets the example of what humility is. The most important man to walk the Earth took on a low view of His own importance so that we could have abundant life. As daughters of a humble King, we can take back our humility and know that this is the example that God desires for us to walk in.

Philippians 2:7-8 says, *"Instead, he gave up his divine privileges; he took the humble position of a slave and was born as a human being. When he appeared in human form, he humbled himself in obedience to God and died a criminal's death on a cross."*

Why do you think it is important to walk in humility?
What example does Jesus set when reading Philippians 2:7-8?
Why are we called to mirror the way that Jesus walked?

DAY 2

How often have we wanted to pick up our rights and fight back? How many times have we wanted to defend ourselves and speak up for something that matters to us? As I ask these questions, I also wonder how Jesus felt. There were times when He was mocked, when He was tempted, and when He was called something that He was not. However, his humility allowed Him to fight back the best way. He did not have to argue or prove a point. His humility spoke for Him. As we journey through taking back our pearls, let us be motivated to allow humility to speak before our emotions or actions.

What misconceptions, if any, do you have about humility? Why is it important to be quicker to respond from humility than from our emotions in the moment? (James 1:19)
Have you responded in humility when you felt people attacked you? Why or why not?

DAY 3

If we are not real with ourselves, we can adopt this mindset of false humility. When we are chasing after the wrong things and carrying offense and unforgiveness then we can put on a fake identity of humility. Instead of letting God lead us, we allow our flesh to take control.

When we walk in humility then we are being led by the Holy Spirit and our flesh has no place to reside there. I remember meeting a person and they said how humble they were yet their actions were so far from that. Humility is that attribute that many of us say that we want, however, our actions can show if we are walking in humility or not. Humility is not an outfit that we take on and off but we should aim to be clothed in it. I Peter 5:5 says, *"All of you, clothe yourselves with humility toward one another, because, "God opposes the proud but shows favor to the humble."*

Have you ever taken on this mindset of false humility?
What is the problem when we are being led by our flesh?
Why is it important for us to wear humility in ALL seasons?
What does I Peter 5:5 push us to do?

DAY 4

Before I experienced the love of Jesus, I was in a very low place. It was a season of my life where I knew that I needed to go higher. My higher place was finding Jesus Christ. Not only was it my higher place but it was the highest place that I would experience. Regardless of the good and bad that I experience in this world, the depth of God never changes. (Hebrews 13:8)

As we are called to go through highs and lows, we can never forget that Jesus will always be our higher place. Humility allows us to see that we need to depend on Jesus. As God opens doors for us, we still have to know that there is no greater door than the door that leads to His throne. That is our high place that we can humbly go to whenever we need to.

What would you consider to be your highest place? Be honest with yourself?

Do you see Jesus as being your highest place? If so, what does this mean for your humility?

Why is it important that we know that we can humbly go to God whenever we need to?

DAY 5

As daughters, our Father wants us to take back our humility when it comes to the way that we treat people. Sometimes the people that we meet today are struggling with things that we overcame yesterday. This means that we can't treat people in a way that they are beneath us because they don't look like the current us. We have to remind ourselves that we all have overcome and are still overcoming something. In this take back season, I want you to be intentional to value others in spite of where they might be right now.

Paul encourages us to not be vain but instead to operate out of humility. It is in humility that we can show others that they are valued. Philippians 2:3 says, *"Do nothing out of selfish ambition or vain conceit. Rather, in humility, value others above yourselves."*

How do you tend to treat people who battle with the things that you have overcome?
What does Philippians 2:3 mean to you?
At times, why can it be hard to value others above yourselves?
How can you be more intentional to do so?

DAY 6

Pride can creep into our thoughts. God gives us power and authority. He does not give us pride. We can see many people who are elevated into different roles that can begin to operate in humility and later can change to operate out of pride. Since pride esteems the person above others, it leads to disgrace. I am not saying to not value yourself but I am saying that when we carry an inordinate or unrealistic view of ourselves then we are operating from pride. Pride is self-seeking and self-pleasing. We want to be the example of women who value ourselves without elevating ourselves to be better than another or even God. Pride divides but humility sticks.

Proverbs 11:2 says, *"When pride comes, then comes disgrace, but with humility comes wisdom."* In what ways has pride crept into your thoughts?

What is the connection between humility and wisdom?

Why is it important for us to be an example of how humility sticks or brings people together? How can you be that glue in your family and your friendships?

DAY 7

REFLECTING

I do not want us to label humility as being timid but I do want us to stay in a posture where we lay our desires and our emotions down at the feet of Jesus. It is a surrender where we give Him all that we have been conditioned to carry. It is a posture that says to the Lord, "I need you!"

James 4:10 says, *"Humble yourselves in the sight of the Lord, and he shall lift you up."* When we are humbled in the sight of God then He will lift us up in the way that HE sees fit. Do not look at humility as the world does. See it from the view of God. Humility might seem as a weakness, but God's strength is perfected in us when we are humble. It takes His strength to operate in humility.

Do you have moments in your life when you feel that humility shows timidity? If so, where has this stemmed from?

Have you ever humbled yourself in God's sight as stated in James 4:10? Is this the posture that you always take? Why or why not?

What does surrender look like for you? Are there still things that you are still carrying that God has asked for you to give up? What steps can you take to do so?

TAKE BACK YOUR PEARLS

DISCIPLINE

We had a home birth with our second daughter and I remember the doula educating me on the type of stretches and breathing techniques that would help my body relax during the labor process. I had never had a home birth before, however, she had home births with her children and also helped many women to deliver their own sons and daughters through the natural process. Nevertheless, the days and the weeks prior to giving birth, I began to remember the stories of other mothers who learned these methods and relaxation techniques. There were the moms who shared that once they went into labor, many of the breathing and relaxation methods were out the window. In a similar way, this is what can happen in the area of our discipline as believers. We can read Scripture and we can watch sermons and we can study through devotionals; however, if there is no true discipline then when we are in a challenging situation then we can throw out the window what God has given us to keep in our hands. As 'take back' women, we have to be able to take back our discipline to stand knowing that when something seems too hard to bear, we have to hold on to the Word of God and the peace of God even tighter. I am not saying that all childbirth is the same and that doulas will work every time and that the experience for whatever we might endure will always be a walk in the park. However, I am saying that just as we need discipline in our natural bodies, we also need discipline in our spiritual bodies as well.

During a challenging season that my husband and I were in, we asked God to show us the area that he desired for us to be disciplined in. He showed us two. He showed us that he wanted us to be disciplined in our prayer life and in our giving. During this season of our life, we were having a home birth. Our insurance did not cover the birth and we also were in the process of trying to fix our credit and pay down debts. However, God did not give us a disclaimer saying, "increase in your prayer life and the area of giving once your bills are paid and the baby comes."

God had wanted us to be disciplined even in those trying moments. We had to learn to be obedient and to discipline ourselves in the very things that God told us to do. Prayer and giving became a big discipline in our home. We prayed when it was naturally inconvenient and we gave out of what we did not have. We sowed into God's work and God's people. Our credit didn't get better and our debts did not go down, however, we continued because of our discipline. As it came close to our second daughter being born, we saw why God had urged us to grow in our prayer and in giving. The night before her birth, I began to feel a shift in my body. It was extremely late, so while everyone else was sleeping, I was up asking God for peace to get me through this birth. This particular pregnancy was a journey where fear had seeped its way into my mind early on so that night I was disciplined enough to pray in faith. As the late hours turned into morning, I called the midwife and shared with her about my physical discomfort. When she came to the house and checked me, I was seven centimeters dilated. Seven, which became the name for our third baby. As I was going through labor, as I shared earlier, I had my doula there encouraging my husband to help my areas of breathing and relaxation as my body tensed up. During labor, I experienced contractions, however, I continued to relax my body through breathing as trained by my doula and encouraged by my husband. Shortly after my water broke, I began to feel pressure. Once this pressure came, I began to feel as if this was too hard for me to do. As I was going through these thoughts, I heard the midwife tell me to reach my hand down and feel her head. Once I felt how close I was, I gave three pushes and she came out. I did not feel any pain as she came through the birth canal. When she came out, I grabbed her and held her in my arms in awe of the miracle of God. I know some women do not get to this process of labor, and so each time that I can witness this, I do not take it for granted. While praising God for this blessing, our daughter takes one breath and stops breathing. As I am holding her closely in the tub, she begins to fall limp in my arms and turn blue. We were not at a hospital and did not have all of the medical staff on site that could handle this type of situation, so the midwife called 911. The thing is, before she called 911 she told my husband to start to pray. As we begin to pray, the ambulance pulls up and the midwife tells her assistant to send them away because our baby girl began breathing as they entered our driveway. I know that every experience is different and this is not always the outcome for some children and some mothers and life in general. However, we still have to be disciplined enough to pray. God is in control and he has orchestrated things out for his glory but he wants us to be partakers in that as well. God orchestrated the midwife, the doula, and my husband and I being in position to pray and declare the promises of God over her life and he worked it in His way. We paid out of pocket, however, other people who were in that bathroom were able to witness the power of prayer. My husband was able to cover me and assist me because we need other people alongside us to help us walk in discipline so that even when it gets tough, we still keep going. Discipline is so important even when the outcome might not be as we want it to. That does not mean that we discontinue disciplining ourselves. We cannot throw away what God is impressing on our hearts because your discipline is not just for you. It is for others around you to be a witness to. The breathing techniques took time to learn, however, I needed to discipline myself to know how to relax my body and I also needed prayer to know that God's peace is the ultimate calming method. However, if I never would have had a home birth or a doula, which we could not afford, they would have never seen the power of God in this way. Your discipline matters.

And sometimes if we don't check ourselves, we can mix up discipline with false obedience where we are following God up until a certain point so that he can perform a breakthrough for our own gain. What happens with that is that the minute that the breakthrough comes our way then we will go back to our old ways. However, I learned that discipline is not just about training oneself to obey but training one's heart and Spirit to be more like Christ. Yes, the season was challenging. Yes, it hurt and was hard and even felt lonely. However, I would rather choose to be disciplined in God than to be trained without Him. We have a good Father who works in so many areas when we learn the true art of discipline. Through this process, we learned to trust God with different areas of our life and we are seeing the fruit of that discipline today. You will feel attacks and experience different trials but you will also live in God's peace. When we go through the trials, as Jesus says in John 16:33, we are still called to be disciplined in Him. When we do then we can operate from a peace that calms us enough to hold onto what He gives us even tighter and not throw it out of the window. John 14:27 says, *"Peace I leave with you; my peace I give you. I do not give to you as the world gives. Do not let your hearts be troubled and do not be afraid."* This peace is only what God can give but in order for us to not allow our hearts to be troubled, we need to be disciplined towards the will of God for our lives so that our obedience and desire to follow God does not come and go but instead it is our heart's desire.

"Whoever heeds discipline shows the way to life, but whoever ignores correction leads others astray."

DAY 1

As a runner, when I think of discipline, I think of the times where I had to run and workout. However, that was not the only thing that I needed to do. I also had to eat healthy and mentally prepare for every race that I ran. Sometimes we see discipline as how we train on the outside. I want us to take a look at those areas of discipline that we need to take when no one is looking.

Matthew 6:1 says, *"Be careful not to practice your righteousness in front of others to be seen by them. If you do, you will have no reward from your Father in heaven."*

When you think of discipline, what other words come to your mind?

Why is it important to be disciplined?

How can you ensure that you are disciplined on the outside as well as the inside when it comes to your walk with Jesus?

DAY 2

It is a beautiful thing to read Scripture and have an understanding of what God is saying to us through His Word. It is even better when we can take His Word and apply it to our lives, especially in those moments when it seems challenging. James 1:22 says for us to be doers of the word and not just people who hear the word. When we apply what we read, then we can see real transformation take place in our faith walk.

Are there times when you read God's word but do not apply it to the different areas of your life? What do you think is keeping you from doing so?

In what ways is God asking you to apply His word to your daily life?

Read James 1:22 again and write down how this applies to different areas of your life?

DAY 3

Spiritual discipline is something that I want to encourage us to Take Back in this season that we are in. We bought a Peloton a few months back. On that bike, I can keep track of the times that I work out along with the input, energy, and time that I put in. I can also see calories that I lost and the pounds that have gone away as a result of what I put out through my workouts. In a similar way, when we are spiritually disciplined then that means that our time spent with our Father takes priority. How we react and respond would be a reflection of the time that we have spent with Him and how His Word has permeated our hearts. We are changed in the presence of God. I encourage you to make sure that His discipline sets a priority above everything else.

Read Matthew 6:33. Now, think about your daily routine or schedule. How much time are you spending alone with God? What are some areas that take away your time that you spend with your Father?

When we are in His presence then we are changed. In what ways has God changed you?

DAY 4

Have you been believing for something that has yet to happen? Maybe you have been standing on God's promises and have been praying and fasting and still have not seen that prayer answered. If that is the case, I encourage you to keep going!

Colossians 4:2 says for us to continue steadfastly in prayer. For me, this took being disciplined in my prayer life to continue to pray even if I did not see it. As I became more disciplined, my prayer life reflected more of the heart of God than the heart of my own desires.

"Be persistent and devoted to prayer, being alert and focused in your prayer life with an attitude of thanksgiving."
Colossians 4:2 (AMP)

What are some things that you have been praying for that God has yet to answer the prayer?
Do you believe that what you are praying for is aligned to God's will?
What does Colossians 4:2 mean for your prayer life?

DAY 5

I can almost guarantee that there is someone who is looking at your discipline. They are looking to see how you will follow after the heart of God rather than the ways of man. It will be challenging and you will be tested; but I encourage you to be the example. Matthew 5:16 encourages us to be that light so that God will be glorified.

When it comes to discipline, training and consistency need to be present. Even greater than those, we have to have trust. We need to trust that our Trainer, who is Jesus, is leading us to the direction that we need to go into. As I learned to trust God with discipline, then I saw that I was much better in His discipline than I was in my own.

Who are some people that are looking at your life?
Are you showing them that you are disciplined in your walk with God? In what ways?
Do you fully trust Jesus? Why is trusting Jesus important for us to walk in the discipline that He desires for us to flourish in?

DAY 6

With discipline, there will be times when you might begin to feel overwhelmed. There might also be some moments where you feel like you are training all alone. I want to encourage you to continue to move forward with God's peace. Do not quit training, do not stop walking in disobedience, but instead go forward with the love and the peace of God. Just like a muscle, it is necessary to exercise our discipline for it to grow and stand on the peace of God as we get stronger in it.

John 14:27 says,

"Peace I leave with you; my peace I give you. I do not give to you as the world gives. Do not let your hearts be troubled and do not be afraid."

Are there ever any moments where you feel that you are alone when it comes to your discipline?

Are there people in your life that can help you walk out your discipline?

There may be moments when it seems easy to throw in the towel as you discipline. How can John 14:27 encourage us not to?

DAY 7

REFLECTING

In 1 Corinthians, Paul talks about disciplining his body and bringing it to God's subjection. We can look at this at the things that we eat or consume. I want us also to look at it as the things that we take in such as the lies and the fears of the enemy. I also want us to think about any ways that we are living that are not acceptable or pleasing to God. This could be the words that we speak, gossip, slander, or even how we treat our bodies. Be honest with where you are and help God to lead you down the correct way.

1 Corinthians 9:27 (AMP) says,

"But [like a boxer] I strictly discipline my body and make it my slave, so that, after I have preached [the gospel] to others, I myself will not somehow be disqualified [as unfit for service]."

How does 1 Corinthians 9:27 speak to you?

Paul says that he makes his body his slave. What does this mean for you?

Regardless of our titles, we are called to talk about our Father and what He did on the cross for us. Why is discipline needed as we spread the good news?

TAKE BACK YOUR PEARLS

OBEDIENCE

Many people would tell me that my oldest daughter was one of the most obedient children that they knew. She would listen and would not talk back. She would do what was asked. I joke and say that God knew what I needed being a college mom who was unmarried and still figuring out life. Nevertheless, I agree that she was obedient. However, what I loved about her obedience was that it was not rooted in fear but rather stemmed from a love and a trust to heed the voice of those who she knew to listen to. It is not saying that she was not scared of the consequences but she did obey out of a love that understood the consequences of her disobedience.

I believe that all of us walk in obedience, however, we need to be able to know if that our obedience is either towards God or towards the enemy. Romans 6:16 says, *"Don't you know that when you offer yourselves to someone as obedient slaves, you are slaves of the one you obey—whether you are slaves to sin, which leads to death, or to obedience, which leads to righteousness?"* We offer ourselves every single day, and many times without realizing that we do. Since we do this, we need to be able to determine whether we are being a slave to sin or being a slave to obedience. Only one will lead to righteousness. Matthew 6:24 declares that we cannot serve two masters so we need to make sure that we are serving the right one. If we are being obedient to God then our obedience leads to something greater than what the world can give us. The world gives us temporal pleasure but God gives us an eternal reward. What my daughter knew was that when she was obedient to the right person and the right things, then the fruit of it was greater for her in the long run. In addition, she was not just obedient to anyone. Instead, she discerned at a young age who was from God and who was not.

Taking back your obedience means that there might be some things that you will stop doing and some places that you might stop going to. That is okay. I Samuel 15:22, tells us that it is better to obey God than to sacrifice or give some things up. We can sacrifice our time and our finances for people and ministry, however, if we are not obeying God by submitting our lives and our heart to Him then we cannot walk in full obedience. Instead of looking at Saul and his faults, some of us need to listen to the Samuels in our lives that are pushing us to walk in obedience. God wants us to see the fruit from obedience so it is not just for our now but it is also for our tomorrow and to encourage the people looking up to us. How often have you been hurt by someone disobeying you and listening to someone else that led them down a wrong way? When we are looking out for their best interest and are encouraging them in a better way than the other person then it hurts when they choose not to listen to the right voice. Now imagine how God feels. When we are submitted to our inner me and our flesh and others more than we are submitted to God then we can begin to obey things that God never wanted us to obey in the first place. When that happens, we are making those things idols because we are becoming more influenced by them than we are by God. I know that we can think of idols as visible things like the golden calf in the Bible from the time of Moses. However, I want you to be alert enough to know that idols can exist in the form of anything that you place over your obedience to God. The Bible does not lie when it says that we cannot serve two masters. Even when looking at social justice and equality from the worldview, I have seen how it can surpass the viewpoint of God at times. When we are led by our emotions and our feelings then we can tend to pick up our rights and our own justice system and put down God's laws. I am not saying that we cannot get passionate but we need to do a heart check and a self-check to determine what and who our passions are submitted to. His ways will always be higher and when we adopt an obedient mindset then our viewpoint and our response will be higher as well.

When we look at the first two forms of obedience as shown in the commandments, we see that the first is to love God with all of our heart and the second is to love our neighbor like oneself. If we can be honest with ourselves and begin there, do we have this foundation of obedience? Can we say that we love God with all of our heart? If we say yes, then we follow His will over our own and submit our ways to His ways. If we say that we love our neighbor like our own self then that means we love even when they don't love and we extend a hand even when they will not take it. These commandments have to be our foundation for obedience because God said these are the greatest commandments. He showed the greatest example when He went to the cross for the people who would be the same one who sent Him there. It was His love and obedience that took Him there and it was His love and obedience that kept Him there. Obedience to God will always be founded in love and that is why we should desire to be a slave to him then a slave to anything that is not him. He loves us and desires for our obedience to be out of a love for Him because it was Him who first loved us.

"If you love me, you will keep my commandments."

DAY 1

When obedience is rooted in love then we can understand that where God takes us is never away from His love or purpose. When we are obeying out of love it is not that we should not know the consequences to our actions when we don't but it is that we have a love and a reverence for the person leading us. God wants to lead us in the right direction so we should love the fact that our Father wants us to be obedient to His ways because they are higher than our own.

Isaiah 55:9 says,

"As the heavens are higher than the earth,
so are my ways higher than your ways
and my thoughts than your thoughts."

Are you obeying more out of love or more out of fear? Why or why not?

Do you believe that God wants us to revere Him honor through our obedience?

As you read Isaiah 55:9, think about the ways that God has proven to you that His ways and thoughts are higher than yours.

DAY 2

We will either be obedient to sin or righteousness so we need to be intentional to follow behind God's righteousness than our own flesh.

Romans 6:16 says, *"Don't you know that when you offer yourselves to someone as obedient slaves, you are slaves of the one you obey—whether you are slaves to sin, which leads to death, or to obedience, which leads to righteousness?"*

Why is it important for us to be obedient to righteousness?
What is the result of being obedient to sin?
Dwell on Romans 6:16.
What does this verse mean to you? In what ways can you take back your obedience and walk in the righteousness that God wants for your life?

DAY 3

The world will produce temporal pleasures and these pleasures will fade away. I remember the times when I was so hungry. Those times where I fasted or haven't eaten for hours can seem challenging. I want to eat everything in sight. However, when I do end up eating or breaking my fast, I realize that I was not as hungry as I thought. In fact, I realize that I could have held off even longer. Sometimes this is us with temporary satisfaction. It will satisfy us for the moment but will not fulfill us. Our obedience to God comes with eternal satisfaction, not a temporary one so let us follow 2 Corinthians 4:18 and fix our eyes on what is eternal.

What are some things in your life that you have taken pleasure in that have satisfied you only for the moment?
Why is it important to know when we need to push a little harder through our obedience? What takes place when we do?
Think about your knowledge of who God is. What things do you appreciate about your relationship with Him that you know will not fade away?

<u>DAY 4</u>

I Samuel 15:22 says,

"Does the Lord delight in burnt offerings and sacrifices
as much as in obeying the Lord?
To obey is better than sacrifice,
and to heed is better than the fat of rams."

This verse shows us that the Lord delights more in our obedience than in what we have given up. Sometimes we look at what we give up as the idol but Jesus wants to see our obedience more than what we have to sacrifice.

List out some things that you have sacrificed over the years. Do you believe that these things are more important than your obedience? Why or why not?
Do you dwell more on what you have sacrificed and given up than in what God has done for you?
Why do you think that the Lord does not delight in offerings more than in our obedience?

DAY 5

God does not want us to have idols. Idols keep us from keeping Him as our first love. When we are more focused on other things than God, then that focus can become our god. When we are more submitted to people or our flesh than to God then those things or people become our controllers. When we are more led by our social rights more than the rights of Jesus then those rights are also idols. Let us prioritize our obedience to God first so that everything that we do comes from the mindset and heart that He comes first and is loved first. Jonah 2:8 says, "*Those who cling to worthless idols turn away from God's love for them.*" We don't want to turn away God's love, instead we want to run to it.

Why does God not want us to have idols?
What are some idols that you have had over the years? Why is it important to lay those idols down?
How can you make sure that you are daily submitted to God and not your rights or your emotions?

DAY 6

Matthew 22:36-38 says,
"Teacher, which commandment is the greatest in the Law?" 37 Jesus declared, 'Love the Lord your God with all your heart and with all your soul and with all your mind.' This is the first and greatest commandment."

When Jesus was asked by an expert what was the greatest commandment, His response was to love God with all of our heart and soul and mind. With this love, it is not halfway or self-seeking. It requires us to be all in. Our love for God, shows in our commandments that we keep to Him.

Are you all in with your love for God? How do you know? During different seasons of your life, were there any barriers that keep you from loving all of God? What were they? Why do you believe that loving God with all of our heart and soul and mind is the greatest commandment? Why is it important for you?

DAY 7

REFLECTING

Our love for God shows in our commandments that we keep to Him.

John 14:15 says, *"If you love me, keep my commands."* If we love God then we should not have a problem with obeying what He says.

God is not like a man where He wants us to obey Him just because. Instead He is a Father that wants you to be the best daughter that you can be. He wants to guide you in all things!

How can you keep God's commandments?
Do you believe our obedience shows God that we love Him?
Think about your relationship with your earthly father. Write about it. Now compare it to your relationship with Jesus? Are there any limitations? How has knowing Jesus changed your view of fatherhood?

AUTHORITY

I have taught on the subject of history for a number of years and throughout my years of teaching, this concept of authority is a topic that is generally brought up. Throughout the rise and fall of empires, the implementation and the abolishment of slavery, the functions of governments, and the creation of laws; there have been many different factors that have influenced or even distorted the true meaning of authority. Even within the body of Christ, there have been some misconceptions about what authority is and who has it. Where we need to start is knowing that God is the ultimate authority. If we are enabled to walk in authority then it is only because God has allowed us to.

Naturally, there are roles and jobs that people are given that enable them to walk in that particular sphere of authority. When we look at the authority of God in Romans 13:1, Paul tells us that the authorities that exist are established by God. Walking in true authority means that we first have to submit ourselves to the One who establishes it in the first place. Once we do this then we can walk in authority that is not just based on our strength but that is backed up by God.

God wants us to walk knowing that He gives us authority. When we take back our authority, we are taking back what God gave us to keep that we may have given away or that other people may have taken from us. Although this might seem hard, we do not have time to waste misusing or not using the authority that God has given us. A few years back, I shared a message on Luke 10 and how the Lord appointed over seventy to go out and spread the gospel. As the chapter continues, Luke 10:19 says, *"I have given you authority to trample on snakes and scorpions and to overcome all the power of the enemy; nothing will harm you."* What took place was that God first appointed the 72 and then later He says that He has given them authority. God didn't just give us power but He gave us authority to overcome the enemy's scheme. He gave us authority that nothing will harm us. His authority enables us to move as He urges us to go. The beautiful thing is that God backs us up and gives up what we need to trample over those things that might attempt to trip us up. The key is to identify that we need God because it is His authority that enables us to move in a way that we cannot do in our own strength. When a miracle happens or a breakthrough takes place and God uses us to have a hand in that occurring, then we can take the focus off of ourselves and what we can do in our limited power. As children, we are heirs of God's authority, and if we are not aware of that authority because we are unsure of who we are, then we delay walking in the true power that comes with our identity in Christ Jesus. When we know that the authority that we are given is one that we could not create or manufacture ourselves, then we should have a desire to want to grow closer to the source that gives us this authority.

The example of Jesus in John 10 gives a picture of how he walked in the authority that God gave him. Walking in authority doesn't mean being the loudest in the room or acting like the most intimidating person. Walking in authority means that you get your instruction to go and then you submit yourselves to the direction that the instructor is telling you to go in. Walking in authority does not mean that what you say goes but it does mean that what He says goes. Taking back your authority means first taking back your knowledge of knowing where your authority comes from. In John 10:18, Jesus says that he has the *"Authority to lay it down and authority to take it up again. This command I received from my Father."* Jesus was stamped with this authority. He had the ultimate authority and His authority was rooted in obedience. We have seen numerous accounts where people who are in authoritative roles abuse their power and can use it as a means to harm others or mistreat others. However, even when the devil tried to tempt Jesus in the wilderness, Jesus could have used his power to show the devil up. However, He did not allow what He could do to override what God told him to do. As we walk in our authority, there are many things that we could do but we have to ask ourselves if God told us to. We have to be real with ourselves and make sure that our authority is being backed by the One who created it and gave it to us in the first place. We have to be able to know when we are stewarding our authority so that it is not becoming a form of abuse and control. We also have to know how to use it because we have been given authority to tread over serpents and that means that our authority has weight to it and we don't have time to waste it. Ephesians 6:12 says, *"For our struggle is not against flesh and blood, but against the rulers, against the authorities, against the powers of this dark world and against the spiritual forces of evil in the heavenly realms."* We are not battling against flesh and blood and what we see but are warring against spiritual forces and the powers of darkness. This isn't a play fight! This is a spiritual war that we have to show up prepared for. We have to show up being backed by the authority of God because in our own strength we will be defeated. We might think we have won, but in reality, we are taking losses after losses when we don't come to the fight prepared. As take back women, let us take back our authority, which is fueled by our obedience to God, so that we can walk in the ways that He desires us to walk in and think in the way that He desires for us to think in. His ways are higher than what our finite mind could decipher.

"I have given you authority to trample on snakes and scorpions and to overcome all the power of the enemy; nothing will harm you."

DAY 1

Some of us have experienced firsthand the abuse of a person's authority. This can be a hurtful place for some of us. However, I want you to take a look at the authority that God walked in. His authority was the hope that opened the door for us to be adopted into His kingdom. He establishes authority and He calls us His! We can trust His authority because it is not like man's. Jeremiah 17:7 says that we are blessed when our trust and our confidence is in him.

Have you experienced authority that was abusive?
Why can this type of authority leave people hurt and broken?
Since God's authority is pure and stems from love, is it easy for you to trust His authority? Why or why not?

DAY 2

Since we are God's daughters, He has given us authority. However, in order to walk in authority then we need to first walk in submission. When we are submissive to God then our authority is enabled through Him. We cannot walk in authority if it is not backed by God. That is walking in our own might. However, by the Spirit of God, He enables us to walk in His authority as we are submissive to His will.

Why is submission important as it relates to authority?
Why is God's authority better than our own might?
Are you walking in the authority of God's power or your might?
Is this the case for some areas in your life?

DAY 3

We have the authority to overcome the power of the evil one. This is not a playable type of authority. This is an authority that encourages us to know that we can trample over the enemy through the power of God.

Luke 10:19 says, *"I have given you authority to trample on snakes and scorpions and to overcome all the power of the enemy; nothing will harm you."*

Do you believe you walk in God's authority?
Why is God's authority something that we need to have full access to?
After reading Luke 10:19, what does it speak to you? Are you intimidated by having this authority? Are you motivated to walk in it more?

DAY 4

As we walk in authority, it does not mean that we need to be the loudest person in the room. Walking in authority means that we have the knowledge to know where our authority comes from. Proverbs 2:6 says that the Lord gives wisdom. Jesus was not the loudest but His words were powerful because they stood on truth. He wants us to walk in His truth. His authority shows the truth that He speaks to us in our daily communion with Him. He did not have to be the loudest because His actions spoke even louder. Think about how you use your authority and decide whether you will define your authority by the level of your voice or by the level of your actions.

Why do people equate being loud with being authoritative? Why is this not the case?
What are some examples of how Jesus walked in His authority?
How have you exercised God's authority that is within you?

<u>DAY 5</u>

Just because you do not pray like another or speak like another person who you might look at as more called than you, does not mean that you do not carry God's authority.

God can use any one of us for His purpose and for His glory. Even when God defined different roles as it related to the church, He was the one who established them to build up His kingdom (Ephesians 4:11-12).

His authority is not confined to this world. His authority is without limits. If you are dealing with a false reality of what authority is then I encourage you to tell yourself that you can walk in it as long as you follow God's voice.

Do you compare your authority to another person who might seem to be more called than you?
If we all get our authority from God, then why would comparing not be beneficial for us?
Do you believe that God can move you to walk in authority that will break generational cycles in your family? How will this look for you?

DAY 6

I can admit that there are some moments in my life where I forget God's authority. I see how the world and society has changed so much and find myself more distracted with what man can do than what God can do. This is why I need to be renewed daily so that I can stand on Scripture and what it says in Matthew.

Matthew 28:18 says, *"And Jesus came and said to them, "All authority in heaven and on earth has been given to me."* Jesus does not have partial authority and His authority is not just in heaven. It is on earth as well.

Are there moments in your life when you lose focus of God's authority? What leads you there?

What are some things that you can take back to your remembrance that can remind you of God's authority?

What does Matthew 28:18 speak to you? Does it give you confidence to know that the authority of Jesus has no limits?

DAY 7

REFLECTING

Ephesians 6:12 says, *"For our struggle is not against flesh and blood, but against the rulers, against the authorities, against the powers of this dark world and against the spiritual forces of evil in the heavenly realms."*

We are in a spiritual battle and we have to know the weapons that we need to use. God gives us authority but He also gives us a strategy to fight. Why is it important to use God's strategy and not our own?

When it relates to what we are up against, do you get discouraged by who we are battling or are you encouraged by who has already won?

How are you preparing for these types of battles?

TAKE BACK YOUR PEARLS

IDENTITY

Throughout the years, my identity had been wrapped up in so many things. Things such as my friendships, my job title, my relationship status, and too many other titles and commitments that I can't recall. To say the least, these titles and roles and labels made up my identity of who I thought I was. Up until a few years ago I didn't really understand my identity as it related to being God's daughter. I thought that I would have to prove something or achieve something major to validate who I was. This concept of being a daughter was distorted for a number of years. In all honesty, I believed that this came from the relationship that I had with my earthly father. Him and I had some differences throughout the years so I tried hard to create an identity outside of that relationship. Because I was hurt, I had to take on identities and masks that would hide the true fact that I was broken and didn't know how to receive the love from a father. When a girl can't receive that love, then her identity can risk being wrapped into so many other things that define her and give her a temporary worth. However, what I learned was that this was pushing me further away from who God said I was. I was creating an identity that was outside of my Heavenly Father because I had been hurt by my earthly one. Over the years, I grew to be rebellious and ungrateful and did not extend grace. I started to become callous in different areas and looked farther from the image that God created me in. I allowed man's disappointments to override the appointment that God set out for me. What I mean by that is that God outlines appointments for us to step into the truth of what he has spoken over us. However, because of the disappointment that might stem in our relationships, we risk showing up late or not showing up at all. We risk allowing man and our own insecurities to be our identity blocker.

I can only imagine how God feels when we take on the identities of everything else except the identity that he has given us and appointed us to walk in. Genesis 1:27, which is penned early in the Bible, tells us that we are made in the image of God. This verse shows us that God, in We form, created our identity in a design that would reflect the beauty of His (their) image. How amazing is that? God the Father, the Son, and the Holy Spirit handcrafted us to look differently in our natural makeup. He made us all to be a reflection of him in the Spirit. He designed us to be like Him and our identity comes from being His. We are not our own and we do not belong to man nor our labels so we have to begin walking in the true identity that was hand-crafted in God's image. I remember during college and how I would go to different parties and different clubs throughout New York and New Jersey. Growing up I liked to dance but was not comfortable wearing short or tight clothes. However, when I went to college I thought it was sexier to wear more revealing clothes that were tighter and shorter because I was introduced to that identity. Imagine how I was trying to dance with clothes that I was not even comfortable in or should not have been wearing. That was not me, however, because I wanted to be accepted or viewed as desirable, I took on an identity that I wasn't even fully comfortable with.

As take back women, we have to do a self-check and be real with ourselves about identities that we take on and off because they can look unlike our Father. When we had our son, we debated naming him after my husband and while I love the name Stefen, we wanted our son to have his own name. I would love for him to grow up and become a pastor like my husband, however, he has to take on the identity that God has given to him. We can train him up in that identity, however, God's identity overrides anything that we can try to place on him. God allows us to be his earthly parents, but He still created our son and our daughters and you and I in His image. This is an image that was orchestrated even before we were formed in our mother's womb and this is an image that should never come secondary to any image and identity that the enemy tries to place on us. This is the season where we need to go to our Father and lay aside everything that was spoken over us that is not who God says that we are. I love life coaches and those who help people to walk out their purpose, however, we need to make sure that we are going to the Giver of life before going to everyone and everything else to figure out who we are and what our identity is. God has already placed it inside of us and when we are not walking it out, you will be just like I was with the short and sexy clothes and walk so uncomfortable. Wear what you were created and wear and do not take it off to fit an identity that you were not meant to carry.

In 1 Peter 2:9-10, it reads, *"For you are a chosen people. You are royal priests, a holy nation, God's very own possession. As a result, you can show others the goodness of God, for he called you out of the darkness into his wonderful light. Once you had no identity as a people; now you are God's people. Once you received no mercy; now you have received God's mercy."* (NLT).

When we are not in God, we do not have an identity. However, as God's people, He gives us our identity because He called us and chose us as His own. You were chosen so even when the world tries to tell you that you are rejected or that you do not matter or that you are an accident; God still chose you and gave you an identity that no one can give you. He has created you!

When we are in Christ, we are a new creation. 2 Corinthians 5:17 tells how the things that are of old pass away because you have been given your true identity. Anything else that you take on is fake or non-existent. When we take back our identity, we are taking back the truth of who we are and throwing away the lies of who we aren't. When I married my husband, I had to take on the identity that came with being his wife. I could not walk in my old ways or marriage would have been even more challenging. In the same way, when we are called to be a new creation and take on the identity of Christ, we cannot pick up old habits and stay the same as before we encountered him. Walking in this true identity should place a desire in you that does not want to walk in the old things that take away from the truth of your identity.

Once you had no identity as a people; now you are God's people.

Over these next seven days, we are going to meditate on Scripture that depicts who we are in Jesus Christ. As you go through each day, meditate on the Scripture and journal the meaning and what ways you might struggle with believing this part of your identity. Then I want you to pray that God will help you see you the way that HE sees you.

DAY 1

YOU ARE LOVED

Ephesians 1:4 (MSG)

"*Long before he laid down earth's foundations, he had us in mind, had settled on us as the focus of his love, to be made whole and holy by his love.*"

Meaning:

Struggles:

Prayer: (You can make your own or use the example below)

Dear Lord,

Thank you for making me the focus of your love. Before you laid any foundation in the Earth, you loved ME! Forgive me for any moments where I forget your love and what it did on the cross for me. You define love and I am thankful that you love me. In Jesus name, I pray. Amen!

DAY 2

YOU ARE A DAUGHTER

2 Corinthians 6:18 (NIV)

"I will be a Father to you, and you will be my sons and daughters, says the Lord Almighty."

Meaning:

Struggles:

Prayer: (You can make your own or use the example below)

Dear Lord,

Thank you for giving me the identity of being your daughter. You have been such a good, good Father to me! Forgive me for any moments where I forget that you care about me as a daughter. In you, I can walk in the confidence to know that you are my Protector. Thank you for loving me and for being a Father to me when I needed you the most. In Jesus name, I pray.

Amen!

DAY 3

YOU ARE FORGIVEN

1 John 1:9 (NIV)

"If we confess our sins, he is faithful and just and will forgive us our sins and purify us from all unrighteousness."

Meaning:

Struggles:

Prayer: (You can make your own or use the example below)

Dear Lord,

Thank you for giving me the gift of forgiveness. Father, I thank you that when I confess my sin to you that you forgive me. Forgive me Father for the times when I do not repent and encourage me to stay at your feet. You love me through my shortcomings and you never condemn. Your love is more than enough and covers a multitude of sins. In Jesus name, I pray.

Amen!

DAY 4

YOU ARE SET APART

Romans 12:2 (NIV)

"Do not conform to the pattern of this world, but be transformed by the renewing of your mind."

Meaning:

Struggles:

Prayer: (You can make your own or use the example below)

Dear Lord,

Thank you for calling me to be set apart. Father, I know that this begins in the spirit of my mind. I apologize for the times when I blend in with the world. I desire to look more like you and understand that my knowledge of things does not come from the world but from you. Thank you for setting me apart for your glory. In Jesus name, I pray. Amen!

DAY 5

YOU ARE CHOSEN

I Peter 2:9 (NIV)

"But you are a chosen people, a royal priesthood, a holy nation, God's special possession"

Meaning:

Struggles:

Prayer: (You can make your own or use the example below)

Dear Lord,

Thank you for calling me chosen. Before the foundation of the world, you chose me. Father, forgive me for the times where I desire to be more accepted by titles or things of the world. Transform my mind and heart to know that I am chosen. You have given me the best clothes to wear as you clothe me in your righteousness and call me yours. In Jesus name, I pray. Amen!

DAY 6

YOU ARE PRECIOUS
Proverbs 3:15 (NIV)
"She is more precious than rubies; nothing you desire can compare with her."

Meaning:

Struggles:

Prayer: (You can make your own or use the example below)
Dear Lord,
Thank you for calling me precious. You say that I am more precious than rubies. You say that I am more valuable than the birds of the air and the lilies of the field. Forgive me for the times that I forget my value. I pray that you will continue to remind me that my value comes from you. Man cannot take away what you have already said was mine. In Jesus name, I pray. Amen!

DAY 7

YOU ARE FREE

Romans 6:18 (NIV)

"You have been set free from sin and have becomes slaves to righteousness"

Meaning:

Struggles:

Prayer: (You can make your own or use the example below)

Dear Lord,

Thank you for setting me free. I once was a captive to sin. However, you call me yours. In you, there is freedom. Forgive me for the moments when I forget the depths of your freedom. Allow me to see that if I am not surrendered to you then I am surrendered to sin. Guide me through this journey as I live in complete freedom in you. In Jesus name, I pray. Amen!

ACCEPTANCE

I am not even going to lie to you. Writing this section on acceptance took me through the battles of acceptance that I walked through for a number of years. At times, we can identify the opposite of acceptance is rejection. However, when asked to dig a little deeper then it can be challenging to understand what acceptance is and what it is not. Growing up, this was a battle for me. It was not because I was not accepted but because I was driven by being rejected. When we battle with rejection, we often think that we are damaged goods or that we have no place. However, I take joy today knowing that my Lord and Savior was known as the cornerstone that the builders rejected. Although He was rejected by man; He was accepted by God. We are accepted by God and not because of anything that you and I did but because when Jesus died on the cross, He died because He loved us and accepted us even when we rejected Him. If we are honest with ourselves, we can identify the moments in our lives where we have rejected God but we can also identify moments in our lives where people have rejected us because we later accepted God. I remember when I committed my life to Jesus Christ and there was a group of people that rejected my walk and did not want anything to do with me because of my step of faith. I could have allowed that to hinder my walk with Christ but I knew that I also had a group of people who accepted me and were rejoicing along with the angels in heaven that this girl who once was lost had been found. Your acceptance is not wrapped up in man but it is wrapped up in the greatest man that has ever walked this earth, who has left you with His Holy Spirit and still walks with you today. Your acceptance is not defined by the college that you get into or do not get into and it is not defined by if you are a wife or a mother at this point in your life. Your acceptance is that God loved you enough to form you to be beautiful in His sight and has given you a purpose and a plan to prosper and will reunite with you on the day of glory when you will meet Him in heaven. God accepted you when He paid the ransom so that the enemy could not have access to your spirit.

You are accepted.

John 10:10 tells us that the enemy wants to steal, kill, and destroy and the biggest thing that he wants to destroy is our knowledge that we are accepted in Christ Jesus. If you need a reminder, in the very first chapter of the same chapter, it says, *"But to all who did receive him, who believed in his name, he gave the right to become children of God."* (John 1:12). You are accepted as a child of God so whether your father rejects you or your mother or your lover, know that God has accepted you as His child and He cares about His children. We need to remind ourselves of this daily! I wear a ring every day and this is not just a reminder to myself that I am accepted by him but it is also a reminder to other people to know that I am not available! Since we are accepted by God, we have to be able to remind the enemy that we are not available! We are not up for grabs because we have already been bought at a price. (1 Corinthians 6:20). We are already taken, we are accepted, and God already has called us His!

Being accepted also means that we have access to certain things. When I was accepted into Rutgers and enrolled in school, I had access to specific buildings and events. When I was kicked out of school for my academics or lost credits because of lack of payment, I had no more access. My keys and badges were not accepted at the places that I once had access to. However, when I got accepted back in and paid my dues, I was not only accepted but upon graduation I became an alumni. I have a stamp of completion because although I got kicked out I was able to find a way back in. When we are in fellowship with God, we have access to certain things so we have to continue to stay in His presence and find our way back to Him if we find ourselves in moments where we leave it. He has given us access and invites us to come into His Holy place and dwell in His presence. In His presence there is fullness of joy and pleasures forevermore and we can experience all of this because we are accepted by Him.

His acceptance also encourages us to accept others when they come to Him. When I came to Jesus, I didn't have it all together. In fact, it was the time that I spent in His presence which enabled me to be more like Him and to get it together. Even though I still don't have it all together today I can say that I have been changed by being in a relationship with him. In the same way, we have to know that God accepts others when they come to Him. His Spirit is enough to do a great work inside of them. Because of this, we have to be careful of those who we might reject. We do not reject the person but we do reject and correct the sin in that person. In Genesis when God was addressing Cain, He said to him, *"If you do well, will you not be accepted? And if you do not do well, sin is crouching at the door. Its desire is for you, but you must rule over it."* (Genesis 4:7). When we do well, we are accepted but when we do not do well then sin can overrule. This is why it is important not to accept the sin. God wanted to save Cain, so he warned him. We should want the same for everyone else. There are sins that we need to address, correct, and reject as we accept the person. Romans 14:1 says, *"Now accept the one who is weak in faith, but not for the purpose of passing judgment on his opinions."* When we accept the one who is weak in faith, we are acting how God did when He accepted us when we were weak and outside of His faith. Let us be the example of accepting what God wants and rejecting what the enemy wants us to take on.

"But to all who did receive him, who believed in his name, he gave the right to become children of God."

<u>DAY 1</u>

Sometimes we can become so focused on being rejected that we overlook that we are already accepted. Being accepted by God sometimes means that we will be rejected by man. However, we can have the peace to know that we are not alone. Jesus was rejected as well. Psalm 118:22 says, *"The stone the builders rejected has become the cornerstone."* However, even though He was rejected, that did not move Him to follow the ways of man. He knew that to get where He was going, He had to face rejection. Where we are going, we will face rejection but we already have God's acceptance.

When you think about the rejection that Jesus had to face, how does it make you feel?
In what ways have people rejected you?
Why is it important that we stand on God's truth, even when others might reject it?

DAY 2

I can imagine how Jesus felt before He went to the cross. John 12 shows us that there were people who were cheering Him along who days later would be cheering for others to crucify Him. This can be our testimony. We have people who were rooting for us in one season and then people who were speaking against us in the next season. As hard as it might be, pray for them. I have experienced this far too often. However, I cannot negate the people who have accepted me and those that God sends to remind me that I am accepted and I am loved.

Have you ever had people who were with you in one season and who have left you in the next? How does this make you feel? Does the rejection of man in your life outweigh the acceptance of who God is to you?

How can you find peace knowing that God accepts you, even when man might reject you?

DAY 3

God accepted you when He paid the ransom so that the enemy could not have access to you. The enemy cannot steal what is not His and God has called you His.

John 1:12 says, *"But to all who did receive him, who believed in his name, he gave the right to become children of God."* You are God's child and you are His daughter.

Why can't the enemy steal what is not His? How does this make you feel as a daughter of God, knowing that you are His?
What do you take away from John 1:12?
What rights do you have as a daughter of God?

DAY 4

Since we are accepted by God, that means that we have to tell the enemy that we are not available. Not only do we have to let the enemy know that, but we also need to remind our inner me that we are not our own.

I Corinthians 6:20 says, *"for God bought you with a high price. So you must honor God with your body."* We were bought with a high price so that means that we are to honor God with our bodies. When people see me, they know that I am married because of the way that I carry myself. When people see us, they should also know that we belong to God because of the way that we carry ourselves.

Have you told the enemy that you are not available lately?
How have you shown this through your actions?
How do you feel knowing that God bought with a high price?
How are you honoring God with your body? When people see you do they see God?

DAY 5

Having access to God means that we also have access to His fullness. Ephesians 3:19 says, *"And to know this love that surpasses knowledge—that you may be filled to the measure of all the fullness of God."* This access is not just for us. This is something that everyone can have if they desire to be in Christ and have Christ dwell in them. Being in the fullness of God should encourage us to want others to be there with us. Leading someone to His love is the best gift that you can give a person. Let your access to God open the door for others to encounter Him as well.

How does it feel when you are in God's presence? How often do you experience being alone with Him?
Why is it beneficial to lead other people to encounter Jesus Christ for themselves?
How often are you leading others to access God? Is there anything that hinders you?

DAY 6

We have to be careful that we are not driven by rejection. In Genesis, we see the result of sin taking over Cain because God did not accept His sacrifice. Although God did not accept his sacrifice, God still cared about Cain making the right decisions so that sin would not rule his life. God cares about your decisions. These decisions can either lead to your destruction or your improvement. Let us choose to do well and clothe our decisions in the truth that God wants us to accept His will for our life.

Genesis 4:7 says,

"If you do well, will you not be accepted? And if you do not do well, sin is crouching at the door. Its desire is for you, but you must rule over it." (Genesis 4:7). According to Genesis 4:7, what happens when we do well?

What can happen when we are driven by rejection?

As you read this account in Genesis, what can you take away from it?

DAY 7

REFLECTING

As we take back the truth that we are accepted by God, let us also take back our desire to encourage others that they can be accepted by Him as well. Romans 14:1 says, *"Now accept the one who is weak in faith, but not for the purpose of passing judgment on his opinions."*

We are called to accept those who might be weak or newer to the faith. In many cases, these people are where we first started. Knowing that we can accept them, how can you personally take the initiative in making them feel accepted?

Sometimes we think that when we accept a person that we are agreeing with their behaviors as well. How can we differentiate between the two and let them know that while we can love them, we might not always agree with their actions?

Being accepted is more than a popularity contest. When we look at Jesus, there were times when His disciple Peter denied Him. Know that when you are walking for Jesus, you will be rejected just as He was. Don't stop walking because of it. Keep on going. Why is it important that you do not stop?

TAKE BACK YOUR PEARLS

SUBMISSION

Submission is one of those words that have often been misused, especially as it relates to us women. It has become so distorted in such a way that there are many of us who will do anything except be submissive. And while I do not believe that we should be submissive to everything or everyone, we do need to be submissive to God. James 4:7 says, *"Submit yourselves, then, to God. Resist the devil, and he will flee from you."* Submission is important because it allows for God to know that we are putting ourselves out of the way so that He can work through us in whatever capacity that he wants us to. The initial part of the verse says to submit to God. As it continues, we are told to then resist the devil. It will be challenging for us to be able to resist the devil if we are not first submitting ourselves to God. When we submit ourselves to God then we can know how to resist the devil. We can talk all day about the negative connotations that come with this word submission. However, if we are not submitted to God then that means that we are submissive to the devil. When we are submitted to God then His authority allows us to be strong enough to resist the devil when he comes. It is amazing how we gain power through submission. It is encouraging to know that we are liberated through our submission to God that the devil flees. He doesn't just walk away, but James 4:7 says that the devil flees! This is because he sees the power of your authority that comes when you submit to God and allow Him to lead you.

Submission is not for the faint. Sometimes we will have to endure some hard moments in our life, however, those hard moments should not determine whether we decide to submit to God or whether we decide to submit to the devil. In addition, when we do not submit to God then that means that we are operating from our flesh. How can we defeat an enemy through fleshly armor? We cannot do it. However, when we submit to the flesh then we have a mind that is of the flesh. Romans 8:7 says, *"For the mind that is set on the flesh is hostile to God, for it does not submit to God's law..."* If we are set on operating in the flesh then we cannot submit to the law of God. When we don't submit to God's law then we are submitting to the law of man and the law of the evil one. We do not have time to submit to our flesh or lean on our own understanding. We need to trust God with our whole heart. Proverbs 3:5-6 urges us not to lean on what makes sense in our own minds. Instead, as we acknowledge God and as we submit to His authority then He will make our paths straight. Have you ever followed behind someone and you have gotten delayed or lost because you were submitted to their direction or leadership? That is because there are people that we sometimes follow and submit to that cannot see where we are going because they have not submitted themselves! In order to lead well, you have to submit well!

Ephesians 5 says that we are to submit ourselves to one another because it is a way that we reverence Jesus Christ. For those of us who are married, some of us might wrestle with the rest of the passage in Ephesians 5 that says, *"Wives, submit yourselves to your own husbands as you do to the Lord. For the husband is the head of the wife as Christ is the head of the church, his body, of which he is the Savior. Now as the church submits to Christ, so also wives should submit to their husbands in everything."* What is being represented here is God's way of order. Just as Christ is the head of the church, the husband is the head of the wife. This does not mean that the wife's worth is less than the husband's worth. It does show that the church is considered the bride of Christ and we know that Jesus gave himself up to cover and protect His bride. In the same way, husbands are supposed to cover their wives and the wives are to submit to the husbands as unto the Lord. When a woman submits to the Lord then God will cover and protect her and give her all sorts of access to him. Submission to God is the most rewarding and loving journey that we could go on. Because of this, it is important to not look at our husbands as the enemy but know that there is a level of order and unity that is unlocked when we walk in submission to God because both the husbands and wives are submitted to God's authority. When one is and the other is not then there is an opportunity for wedges to be created that can build walls up between husband and wife. We have to be willing to walk in submission so that the perfect will of God can be present in our lives as God unlocks places for us to have access to because we first submitted to Him.

Over the next seven days, I want you to take the time to journal or even draw out your thoughts as it relates to submission. I believe that some of us need to take back God's truth of submission. Some of us need deliverance on this topic because it has been widely misused. Do not quit and do not give up. If you feel as if you want to, just know that someone needs you to finish the race so that they can start!

"Submit yourselves, then, to God. Resist the devil, and he will flee from you."

DAY 1

James 4:7 (NIV)

"*Submit yourselves, then, to God. Resist the devil, and he will flee from you.*"

DAY 2

Hebrews 13:17 (NIV)

"Have confidence in your leaders and submit to their authority, because they keep watch over you as those who must give an account. Do this so that their work will be a joy, not a burden, for that would be of no benefit to you."

DAY 3

Romans 8:7 (NIV)

"The mind governed by the flesh is hostile to God; it does not submit to God's law, nor can it do so."

DAY 4

Job 22:21 (NIV)

"Submit to God and be at peace with him; in this way prosperity will come to you."

DAY 5

1 Peter 3:1 (NIV)

"Wives, in the same way submit yourselves to your own husbands so that, if any of them do not believe the word, they may be won over without words by the behavior of their wives,"

DAY 6

Ephesians 5:21

"Submit to one another out of reverence for Christ."

DAY 7

Romans 7:4

"So, my brothers and sisters, you also died to the law through the body of Christ, that you might belong to another, to him who was raised from the dead, in order that we might bear fruit for God."

AFFIRMATION

Although this journey of taking back your pearls through this book is coming to an end, that doesn't mean that your journey stops here.

Over the next six days, I encourage you to affirm yourself and other women around you. What you have taken back and can now carry can also be the key to unlocking things in others around you. Because you moved, now someone else can too!

DAY 1

"I can do what I was born to do!"

God has created a purpose and a plan for your life so fight everyday knowing that you have the power that God has given you to do what He has created you to do!

(Jeremiah 29:11)

DAY 2

"I am enough!"

God has given you the truth to know that you are enough.
When He gave His life so that you could have a new life in Him,
He began a work in you because you are enough.

(Philippians 1:6)

DAY 3

"I am who God says that I am!"

Your identity is wrapped in the truth that you are God's. He calls you chosen and man cannot take away the truth that He has called and seated you in high places.

(Ephesians 2:6)

<u>DAY 4</u>

"I am going to be the best version of ME!"

Too often we see carbon copies but God has called you to be the best version of YOU. You are fearfully and wonderfully made and that needs to be illuminated in the Earth.

(Psalm 139:14)

DAY 5

"I am not a slave to fear!"

Fear has held some of us back for too long. It is time for some of us to take leaps into what God truly has for us. We are going to operate from love and no longer from fear.

(I John 4:18)

__DAY 6__

"I am not alone!"

Too often the enemy makes us think that we are alone. That is a lie. You have brothers and sisters in Christ that want to see you flourish. You also have a God that calls you His daughter. You are not alone and you never will be. The Holy Spirit lives within you and God will never leave His children.

(John 14:16)

Now live in the truth of knowing that what God has for you is for you and that no enemy can take that away!

GOD, INSTILL IN ME

A Poem by Carolyn Grignon (My Mother)

For me, over my life
When sadness and despair
enter my realm
Raise me up to face
whatever it may be
Silence the fears
Dry all my tears
Let me be open to You,
search for You
reach for You only,
It is only then
that I will experience
Your tranquility
and your true will
for my life

TAKE BACK YOUR PEARLS

Made in United States
Orlando, FL
06 September 2023